PRAISES FOR
NO FENCE, NO LIMITS

"In a world where the journey to parenthood
is often marred by silence and stigma, Kelly's
book stands as a beacon of hope and resilience.
This remarkable book courageously delves into
the raw, unspoken struggles of IVF, offering a
profound exploration of both the challenges and
unexpected joys that come when life gives you an
unpredictable path.
Through heartfelt anecdotes and unwavering
honesty, Kelly and husband Jed share the emotional
terrain of infertility and the family/societal pressures
that accompany it. Their story is a testament to the
strength of the human spirit."

Jarrad and Michael Duggan-Tierney,
The Real Dads of Melbourne
Parents to a child born via
international surrogacy IVF

"As someone who conceived naturally with my first two pregnancies and quickly with my third through IUI (on a solo journey), reading Kelly's story has been profoundly eye-opening.

It has given me a deeper appreciation of the pain, challenges, and identity struggles that women and their partners endure when faced with infertility.

While I'm fortunate to have not experienced these hardships myself, I once believed I was well-informed on the subject and had genuine empathy for those navigating such treatments. However, Kelly's deeply personal insights were a heartbreaking reminder that I could never truly grasp the depths of the pain that come with infertility. It made me want to apologise to those I've encountered for ever thinking I understood.

As the reader, I felt Kelly's endless cycle of disappointment. I felt the coldness she suffered, the emotional agony, and the overwhelming suffocation of her own thoughts – as I do sympathise with going through life as a woman feeling as though your body is broken.

I felt her deep yearning for a child of her own, and

when Kelly wrote, "I just wanted it to be my turn,"
I desperately wished for it to be hers too.
This book is an extraordinary read and offers
invaluable insight for those of us fortunate enough
not to be touched by infertility.
It serves as a warm, comforting embrace for those
currently on their own infertility journeys, offering
reassurance that life can still be beautiful and that
our individual stories shape who we are.
Kelly is a true inspiration. By revisiting wounds –
perhaps ones that never fully healed – she offers
hope to those confronting a childless future that
they may have never imagined. Her story is a
powerful reminder that a woman can define her
own path, finding purpose and passion beyond the
roles society has traditionally prescribed."

Sophie Cachia,
Presenter, businesswoman, entrepreneur,
digital marketing expert, and
sports journalist in Australia.
sophiecachia.com

No Fence
No Limits

No Fence No Limits

Designing an Unconventional Life

KELLY DONOUGHER

First published in 2025 by Dean Publishing
PO Box 119
Mt. Macedon, Victoria, 3441
Australia
deanpublishing.com

DEAN PUBLISHING

Cataloguing-in-Publication Data
National Library of Australia

Title: No Fence, No Limits
ISBN: 978-0-648995-70-8
Category: Self-help/memoir/infertility

Front cover photograph by Stef King, www.stefking.com.au

Page 154 photograph by Armelle Habib, www.armellehabib.com

The views and opinions expressed in this book are those of the author and do not necessarily reflect the official policy or position of any other agency, publisher, organisation, employer, medical body, psychological body, or company. Assumptions made in the analysis are not reflective of the position of any entity other than the author(s) — and, these views are always subject to change, revision, and rethinking at any time.

The author, publisher or organisations are not to be held responsible for misuse, reuse, recycled and cited and/or uncited copies of content within this book by others.

This book is not intended to replace any professional advice or diagnose or treat any health or mental health issues. It offers the author's experience and insights around a topic that is often considered difficult to talk about. The journey of infertility is a multi-faceted subject with many differing recommendations and sources. The reader is advised to always seek professional advice and care according to their specific health needs, whether mental, emotional or physical.

Some names and identifying details of others have been changed to protect the privacy of individuals.

To my incredible husband Jed,

As I sit down to write this, my heart swells with gratitude and love for the man who has been by my side for the past 23 years. You have taught me so much, and I am forever grateful for your unwavering support and strength throughout our journey together. Through the ups and downs of life, you have remained my rock, my constant source of love and laughter. I cannot imagine where I would be without you by my side, guiding and cheering me on every step of the way. Your ability to always make me laugh, even in my darkest moments, is a gift that I cherish every day. I still remember that time in Bali when I fell backwards off my pool lounge and you couldn't stop laughing. As I sat there waiting for you to help me, I couldn't help but laugh along with you. Your infectious laughter is just one of the many things that amazes me about you, along with the way you whistle when you're happy and you think no one is listening.

As I write this, tears of joy fill my eyes, but they are quickly replaced with laughter as I think of all the times you have made me laugh hysterically. It's moments like these that make me realise just how lucky I am to have you as my husband. You are an incredible person, my soulmate, and my partner in life. No matter what challenges we face, I know that we will always overcome them together. And through it all, you continue to amaze me with your unwavering love, support, and strength. This book is not just about my story, but about our journey together. A journey filled with 15 years of ups and downs as we tried to conceive a family. The challenges we faced only made us stronger, and it was during this time that I found my true passion as an interior designer.

From starting my dream business to smashing every goal we set, I have come to realise that the fork in the road moment we faced and the path we chose next was exactly where we were meant to be. If you had asked me in my 20s what my future life would look like, I may have painted a picture of a married couple with children, working our way up the ladder in local government. But life had other plans for us, and I wouldn't have it any other way. As we continue this journey together, I am excited to see where life takes us. Because with you by my side, I know that we can overcome any challenge and create a life filled with love, laughter, and endless adventures. I love you more than words can express.

Forever and always,
Your loving wife.

CONTENTS

PRELUDE

To my readers,

   You don't earn stripes for the number of IVF cycles you complete, clinics you see, or children you bear. I am no different from someone who has only done one cycle and becomes pregnant or someone who does 12 and still struggles. We are all on the same highway of fertility treatments, and I want this book to inspire anyone who faces challenges with fertility or uncertainty in life choices.

   This is not your typical self-help guide on how to achieve the life you've dreamt. You won't find a neatly wrapped happy ending with a picture-perfect family on the last page. But that's okay. It's important to see that it's okay. As difficult as it has been to write every line in this book, I needed to do it to inspire and show you that sometimes, out of the greatest adversity and challenges, something truly remarkable can happen. No matter which stage of this journey you may be in, I hope this book ignites your courage to challenge the perception of what your life is supposed to look like, and by doing so, it may also help shape your why. My hope is for you to become the best version of yourself – a version you didn't even know was possible. Whatever version that may be, it's okay.

This is your white picket fence journey, not your neighbour's, sister's, or best friend's. Embrace how your journey starts and ends, whether it includes a family or not. Find your bliss, but above all, remember to always question and challenge yourself every step of the way. I firmly believe that you will be surprised at what the future can hold for you.

Lastly, I want to leave you with this thought: every challenge we face in life sets us on the path to where we are meant to be. And now, at 44 years of age, I finally understand that this is where I am meant to be. I am excited to see what the future holds, and I hope you are too. Thank you for embarking on this journey with me. Let's discover the remarkable together.

With love and hope,

Kelly

INTRODUCTION

"So, do you have any children?"

The woman leaned forward slightly and looked at me expectantly.

I squirmed in my chair and responded with a soft smile. "Not yet." She continued to look at me with this vague expression and before I could help myself, I blurted out, "But we're trying."

Her face transformed into one of sympathy and I immediately regretted confiding that to a stranger.

"Oh, lovely! Don't worry if it takes a while. My husband and I tried for three long months before it finally happened."

I nodded along and took a sip of my drink to help swallow the shame. "How old are your children now?"

She took the conversation from there and I leaned back, content to steer the conversation away.

While I had felt uncomfortable with this conversation at the time, I had absolutely no idea just how much my response to this question would change.

CHAPTER 1

DREAMING FROM BEHIND THE WHITE PICKET FENCE

When we obsess
over the script our
whole lives, we feel
the ending is owed.

*E*veryone has expectations for their life. Whether they are set by society, our parents, our religion, or ourselves, we all are operating through a lens of expectation and convention. It could be that you are expected to become a doctor like your parents, fit into the gender norms of Western society, or take over the family business. Expectations can also be formed from negative or unhelpful assumptions, including beliefs that you fail at everything you do, you aren't smart enough for university, or you must make a six-figure salary to feel happy with yourself.

We all have different constructs of what a successful life looks like, and if we don't live up to that, or *can't* live up to that, we can deal with great amounts of grief and shame over this version of ourselves that we (or the people around us) dreamed up but will never exist. In some ways, the expectations that hit the hardest are usually the ones we have set for ourselves.

The expectation I held for myself, and that was reinforced by my family, was the 'white-picket-fence' dream. I wanted to get married, have kids and be very family orientated while still having a career that fulfilled me. And while some people defy their expectations in a way that allows them to live a life more aligned with themselves, I never planned to be unconventional. I *wanted* this, wholeheartedly and genuinely, and I did everything I could to get it.

✳ ✳ ✳

I was born into the suburbs of Sydney and raised in the bustling 80s where the air was thick with the scent of possibility and ambition. My family, a unit of four, consisted of my younger brother and my hardworking parents. They strived to provide us with the lifestyle they never had, one that was filled with endless opportunities and luxuries. My parents, products of large families, were moulded by a time where the ultimate goal was to find your forever person, get married, have children, and settle down in your own white-picket-fenced home. This was the epitome of the 80s and 90s, a time where societal norms dictated the path to success and happiness.

Growing up, my parents instilled strong morals and values in us. They taught us the importance of hard work, doing the right thing, and being good people. We were raised to believe that if we were good, kind-hearted individuals, good things would naturally come our way. But we also knew that we had to work tirelessly for it. However, I never quite fit into the mould of the typical school kid, teenager, or young adult. I was mature for my age and never quite went with the crowd, often feeling out of place. I know I must have driven my parents crazy at times, but I couldn't help it. I was fiercely independent, and I tended to speak my mind without a filter.

So, I guess you can say I wasn't your typical teenage partygoer, getting into trouble and mischief, but I also wasn't one who had everything figured out post-graduation. I didn't know if I wanted to go to university or TAFE or what subject I would study if I went. I simply didn't have a strong passion for any one field. If you were to read through my old school journals, you'd see that I often went back and forth between wanting to be a teacher or a hairdresser – like every other little girl growing up in the 80s. However, one thing that was always clear about my future was that I wanted to get married, have a family, and live a normal life in the suburbs at a comfortable pace. These expectations stemmed from my upbringing and surroundings, comparisons to family and friends and the world we lived in. I'd imagined that white picket fence story for such a long time that I couldn't even imagine it being another way.

Kinderga... School

Engadine Central

Kelly Wood

When I grow up I want to be :-

Fireman	Astronaut	Mother ✓
Policeman	Soldier	Nurse
Engine Driver	Footballer	Teacher
Doctor	Teacher	Actress

Year 2

When I grow up I want to be :-

Fireman	Astronaut	Mother ✓
Policeman	Soldier	Nurse
Engine Driver	Footballer	Teacher
Doctor	Teacher	Actress

Year 3

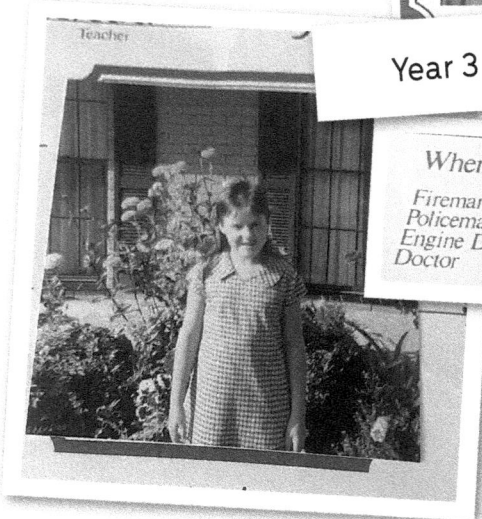

Teacher

When I grow up I want to be :-

Fireman	Astronaut	Mother ✓
Policeman	Soldier	Nurse
Engine Driver	Footballer	Teacher
Doctor	Teacher	Actress

✳ ✳ ✳

When I graduated from high school, my friends were all heading to university and TAFE studying accounting, law or various arts degrees, but I just didn't have that drive. I didn't want to waste countless hours at university and go into debt for something I had no interest in studying. So, I went straight into full-time work as a swim teacher and met my now-husband Jed when I was 20. At this time, I was career driven and worked my way up to run the small swim school, but I also had the view that it had an end point and motherhood was next.

Fast forward to 2005, and I was a young and inexperienced 23-year-old. Having gotten recently engaged, Jed and I ticked off the next item on the list and proudly acquired our first house, inking the contract on the 13th of July (you'll soon notice a recurring theme in our lives surrounding the number 13). Having grown up in Engadine, my childhood home still held a special place in my heart, and so we made the decision to reside in the same suburb to be close to our family. Though it was a modest three-bedroom house with just one bathroom, we couldn't be more thrilled with our purchase. I had already begun planning renovations before we even finished unpacking our boxes.

Engadine was a wonderful place to grow up, and I was

fortunate to have some of my closest friends from school still living in the area. This meant we easily fit into a tight-knit community of friends, and I continued to play soccer with my girlfriends while Jed joined a local team. We were fully immersed in the Engadine gang, attending family gatherings, going on holidays together, and participating in the never-ending cycle of sports that was the norm in the area. I'm sure many families can relate to the hustle and bustle of sports season, a rush from one destination to the next with little time for relaxation. Every Sunday, we would pack up and head out to multiple soccer fields with our friends and family, a tradition that was deeply ingrained in the Engadine culture. If we weren't playing sports on the weekends, it almost felt like something was missing. Our weekend ritual involved the whole tribe, with each family bringing along their prams and toddlers.

Then in 2006, we tied the knot on January 13. And yes, we chose to say our vows on a Friday the 13th. Of course, the assumption when you get married is that you automatically start planning a family. It's laughable how automatic this is, and it's almost always directed at the woman in conversations. Being in this close knit community of our friends and family, this expectation was heavily placed on us; however, we were on the same page. We agreed about wanting to have children young from the very start of our relationship, and now that we were married, we had ticked off the final item on the list. We had our home, loved where we lived and we really just wanted to cement our lives together with a baby.

At the time, I'd never thought 24 was too young to start having a family, as I had always envisioned us as young parents, following the same path as everyone else in terms of family life. Get married, have kids, and settle into the typical suburban life with a white picket fence. That's what I grew up believing, seeing my parents, friends, and relatives all do the same. *Why would I be any different from them, my own family and siblings?*

As for work, I had never planned on a huge career, and every month that I wasn't pregnant was another month that I continued to work in an environment that was often unhealthy – I was plagued with workplace issues and staff challenges daily. I didn't see any other path besides becoming a mum and leaving this workforce behind. At the same time, I was fiercely nervous about what that would look like financially. *Could we actually afford for me to be off work, how long could we sustain one income, how would we juggle life?* The organiser in me planned meticulously, right down to every cent we would need, what we could claim and how life might look with one income for the time being. The financial instability terrified me. We were in the early stages of our first mortgage, and we knew that we would outgrow it quite quickly. But we also wanted this and were willing to work through any challenges together.

I remember those early days being filled with such excitement, fully believing that one day I would be like all my friends who brought their kids to the weekend games, even though I wasn't even pregnant yet. I couldn't help but plan for how I would juggle sports, pregnancy, and future children. (I tend to think three steps ahead, even before completing the first step – a trait that Jed often describes as a maze, with numerous paths leading to unknown destinations.) I knew it wouldn't be easy, but seeing my friends, particularly Danielle, inspired me. Dan, if you're reading this, know that you were a true inspiration to me during those early days. With three kids, you were a natural and could effortlessly handle the juggle, all while being a true mum at heart. You were always one of those friends I could pick up the phone and call and it would feel like no time had passed. Danielle was having babies like clockwork, and she expertly planned them around the sports season, making her a true rockstar at the juggle. She could look at her husband and be pregnant the following week! I figured Jed and I would be the exact same.

Reflecting on those early years, I am now cringing at my naivety.

CHAPTER 2

THE SHOCK THAT WASN'T IN THE SCRIPT

We might draft our futures in permanent marker, but that doesn't make it unerasable.

We officially started trying to get pregnant a few months after our wedding, and the excitement was palpable. We were blissfully unaware at how important timing was when trying to fall pregnant, and I'd never even been in a conversation or really delved into understanding how you become pregnant. My assumptions and naivety were wild. Equally, I didn't have much of an understanding about infertility. We didn't have anyone in our close circle of friends who had experienced this (that we knew of, anyway). It wasn't common to have these conversations in the early 2000s, and so we went forwards, expecting it to just happen.

In the meantime, my usual weekend routine involved playing my own game before watching the boys' games with the other wives, and we would stand around talking about the kids – or rather, I would listen. Week after week, I hoped I'd be able to announce I was pregnant like one of the girls did month after month. Don't get me wrong, I was over the moon to be able to share this joy with many of my friends and would never begrudge anyone's happiness, but I just wanted it to be my turn.

We literally tried everything to conceive naturally, and I must say that using saliva test kits for ovulation was the most exasperating form of testing ever. I am uncertain if this method is even available anymore, but let's share a laugh, shall we? I don't know about others, but the idea of spitting onto a device to obtain a so-called 'fern-looking image' for ovulation just seemed bizarre to me. No matter what the image showed, I convinced myself it was a fern! I tried it numerous times, set alarms to spit on it at precise times, and even refrained from eating or drinking for 30 minutes prior, but that darn thing never gave me a clear result! And don't get me started on those 'pee on stick' types – they were a literal nightmare. Back in 2006, these were the only options, but I'm certain (and I hope!) there are more effective methods for tracking ovulation now.

We experimented with various methods for over 6 months, and I couldn't help but wonder if it would have been easier if I wasn't working or if Jed wasn't so busy with his job. But we had a mortgage and a lifestyle to maintain, so I had to work. It was always a struggle to take the test at the right time, especially as we navigated the hectic pace of life in Sydney. I'm sure most of you reading this are thinking, "Six months? That's nothing!" Trust me, I look back at this time and laugh at myself too. Anyone going through the journey of trying to conceive knows that 6 months can feel like an eternity, but I also know that it's nowhere near the tough times some face.

During that period, I was willing to attempt anything. As advertisements and commercials inundated the television, it seemed like every turn I took was met with something connected to children – having them, preparing for them, caring for them. My entire existence was completely consumed. I was truly convinced that a mere trip to the grocery store for some vitamins would solve our struggles. We experimented with all different kinds and even dabbled with various diets, reduced our alcohol intake, and made an effort to exercise.

I eagerly anticipated a positive pregnancy test, only to be met with disappointment. I began to question if I would ever become a mother. My friends and family were having children left, right and centre, while I felt stuck in this endless cycle of disappointment.

It didn't help my morale that I was surrounded by children in my personal and professional life – I managed over 4000 children in swimming and recreation programs for the local government, plus I ran a swimming school in summer from my own home – yet I couldn't have my own. The joy of my friends' announcements and the constant presence of children in my life highlighted what I couldn't seem to achieve. It was a difficult pill to swallow, and I often found myself feeling isolated and alone. I felt like my body was failing me, and the emotional rollercoaster was all-consuming. Not being able to conceive was the most puzzling, frustrating and challenging scenario I'd ever experienced. We were tired, bewildered and overwhelmed.

As I reflect on this period of my life, I realise more than ever that I was quite young. It's natural at this stage of life for everyone, but looking back, I see that I was incredibly naive. I didn't know anyone else who was struggling, and that's the thing – no one talked about it. It was almost a forbidden subject, which made the journey even more challenging. I felt like I couldn't share my struggles or, worse, that I was a failure. It's not like I hadn't faced failure before, but this was a brand new sensation. There was a whole new level of disappointment and guilt for Jed, as well. He had a beautiful daughter from his first marriage – she was with us every second weekend – and he was eager to become a father again. I knew being a parent was his ultimate joy in life, something I had yet to experience, and being a step mum came with its own set of challenges as you are a 'kind of' parent to someone who doesn't see you as a parent.

At the start, I would share my struggles with my friends during those conversations on the sidelines. But as the journey became more difficult, I found myself sharing less and less. The constant chatter around me invaded every part of me. It became increasingly challenging to exist amid others' happiness and normal lives, and it was tough to be around conversations about kids' activities, kindergarten enrolment, and upcoming birthday parties. It was hard to constantly hear about their lives and struggles with kids, when all I wanted was to have my own kids and relate to those struggles. However, I can't say I always felt excluded, as I had a great group of friends and had experience working with and teaching children, so I always felt like I had something to contribute to conversations.

At the same time, I was having a lot of conversations that were unwittingly making me feel worse about the situation. I am not writing this to shame my loved ones, but simply to explain that it is difficult to know what to say when experiencing fertility struggles. It's not that they don't mean well, but unless you have been through it yourself, it's hard to understand the right words to say. *Is there even a 'right' thing to say?*

I understand that most people are just trying to offer support and comfort. However, it's important to acknowledge that these well-intentioned words often come from those who have never dealt with fertility issues themselves. In sharing the unhelpful words that were said to me at this time, I hope to provide a light-hearted look into the ups and downs of this journey. Of course, not every moment is humorous, but I hope that others who have gone through this can find some comfort in knowing that they are not alone. Let this be a comical interlude in an otherwise serious and emotional journey.

"It will happen eventually."
Sorry do you have a crystal ball? I didn't know you were God? At least I can uncross all my fingers and toes now, as I roll my eyes back into my head.

"Don't think about it and it will happen."
Sure, real easy, I won't think about it at all. I won't think about the doctor's appointments, daily blood tests, scans, waiting for phone calls and the dreaded two-week wait to find out if you're actually pregnant and this is just the IVF process. There's the whole going it alone, ovulation testing, pregnancy tests each month… yeah don't think about it. Got it! I'll just leave now before I… SCREAM.

"Try this, it worked for me."
Everyone you know has some kind of strategy that worked for them when it took them a whole three months to fall pregnant. I'm not mocking all you fertile people… well yes, I am a little I guess, but here's a few I've heard over the years… Legs in the air after sex, herbal treatments, don't have a hot shower after, morning sex only (!), boxer shorts for hubby (gotta keep those swimmers cool), acupuncture, sex two days before ovulation, sex two days after ovulation, etc., etc., etc…

"I'm sure you will be fine."
We all know this is the saying when they don't know what to say,

and I do feel for our family and friends because most honestly didn't know what to say.

"You're only young, you still have heaps of time."
This one really makes me laugh. Yes, I was young at the time but when you really want to start that family and envision being young parents, every year that rolls by feels like 100.

✳ ✳ ✳

So here I was at 24, navigating being a step mum, trying to have my own child and dealing with this sense of shock that everything wasn't naturally falling into place like it was supposed to. It was a challenging period, to say the least. But through it all, I had my friends and Jed by my side. They were my rocks during this challenging time, and I am forever grateful for their unwavering support and reminders that I was not defined by my ability to have children.

I remember one particular day when I was standing on the sidelines of a soccer field surrounded by my friends and their growing families. I felt a mix of emotions: happiness for them, longing for myself, and a sense of uncertainty about my future. It was at that moment that I made a promise to myself – I would not let this define me. I knew that my worth was not tied to my ability to conceive, and I refused to let it consume me. So, with a deep breath and a determined glance towards the field, I pushed aside my worries and joined in on the cheerful chaos of the game.

Despite my resolve, the journey was far from easy, and the questions still lingered: *Why was this so easy for everyone else? What more could I do? Was I missing something?* But I refused to give up.

NAVIGATING THE SHOCK

When our plans don't tick along as we intended them to, we can often be confronted with a sense of shock. I know I was. I never considered that I would have fertility issues, so when my expectations were suddenly at risk of not being attained, I was faced with feelings of disbelief, numbness, and an inability to process the implications. The planner in me simply just didn't process shock. I hadn't really dealt with this kind of emotion before, and I ultimately had no understanding of how to move through it. I was constantly fighting to understand why this was happening to us. I had this deep ache in my stomach because I knew I didn't have the power to fix it, and I had to adjust all my expectations from a future that I honestly thought was a given.

This feeling can be applied to any kind of expectation. Being rejected from your dream university, realising the career you've wanted to do since you were 10 isn't suited to you, or being broken up with by the person you thought you'd marry – all of these come with a state of shock. What you thought was written into the tapestry of your life in permanent marker has been erased. Sometimes you are the eraser, but other times you're not.

Either way, it can be profoundly destabilising. This disconnect between what you thought 'should be' and what actually is creates a kind of cognitive static. You try to make sense of it: *Why didn't this work out? Did I do something wrong? Was I naive to believe it would?* The mind scrambles to reconcile the narrative you've built with the facts at hand, but the story doesn't add up. It's a bewildering clash between expectation and experience, and your internal compass can feel completely thrown off.

That clash often comes with a strange stillness – emotional, physical, or both. You might feel detached from yourself, like you're watching your life from outside your body. Maybe you're waiting for the shock to wear off, for someone to step in and tell you it's all a mistake. But it isn't. The numbness is your system's way of cushioning the blow, protecting you for the time being.

During this period of shock, it's completely okay if you feel:

- Betrayed by your expectations

- Naïve for thinking it would be easy

- Disoriented, as if you've lost a sense of direction or identity

- Embarrassed or ashamed, even if it's no fault of your own

- Jealous of those whose plans are going smoothly

- Like withdrawing or avoiding people who remind you of what you've lost

- Emotionally numb or unable to cry, even if you want to

- Like you're stuck in a loop, replaying what went wrong

It took me a while to transition out of the shock, and what mainly got me through was evaluating the situation and finding another way I could stick to the script. Sure, it might be adding a few more acts to the play, but I was determined to still get the finale. This might not be the case for you though, as this stage is all about sitting with your thoughts and feelings and identifying how the challenge has impacted the way you see yourself and your future. For me, I knew that no matter what was thrown my way, I genuinely wanted the expectation I had set and knew it was right for me. Therefore, I sought alternative methods, practised gratitude every day, forgave myself for my 'failures', let go of the guilt, and focused on the parts of the script that were still mine to write.

CHAPTER 3

DENIAL...
DETERMINATION...
SAME THING,
RIGHT?

When failure knocks
on the door, denial
answers pretending
everything is fine.

*O*ur next chapter began with a doctor's visit, a series of tests, and a path we never imagined we would have to take. As we embarked on our investigation into why we were unsuccessful in conceiving, we were provided with a comprehensive list of recommended tests from our GP. With each booking, we eagerly followed their instructions. In these circumstances, we often trust that the professionals know best. After all, they are the experts in their field and handle these situations daily.

During my initial round of testing, my pap smear results revealed some irregularities, which was a first for me. As a result, I was advised to have my 'tubes checked'. Despite my lack of understanding, I blindly entered the clinic to undergo the test, assuming it would be a simple scan or at most, another internal examination.

I sat in the bustling clinical waiting room on my own, my heart racing with a mixture of anxiety and anticipation. The sterile smell of disinfectant filled my nostrils, making me feel like I was suffocating. I tried to distract myself by studying the ugly peach coloured walls, decorated with outdated brass-framed pictures and mismatched, worn-out cane furniture. *This must be one of those clinics from the 80s*, I thought to myself with a hint of bitterness. Definitely not my style. Did they not understand how much the environment can affect a person's state of mind? But then again, at least its ugliness distracted me from the fear and uncertainty that consumed me. My usual support system was unable to be by my side, as we were trying to limit the impact on our work, but little did I know I needed their hand-holding more than ever.

I took a deep breath, trying to steady my nerves when I heard a voice call out, "Mrs. Donawa?" I stood up, my legs feeling like jelly as I made my way towards the voice. One day, I told myself, my name will be pronounced correctly. I was led into another sterile and clinical room that was filled with a cast of characters – doctors, nurses, technicians – all with their own stories and motivations. Some kind and compassionate, others cold and distant. But all with the power to impact my life in ways I couldn't even begin to imagine. As I took my seat and waited for the next step, I couldn't help but wonder what the future held. *Will I be able to handle whatever comes my way? Will I find the strength to fight?* Only time would tell.

The petite nurse with her crisp white uniform and perfectly coiffed hair handed me the flimsy gown, her lips curving into a smile as she said, "Change, no underwear needed." My heart started to race, and my palms became slick with sweat. This was not what I had signed up for. I entered the room, shivering in the cold darkness. The sterile smell triggered a wave of anxiety. I could feel my bottom exposed through the slit in the back of the gown, and I couldn't help but think there must be a better design for this humiliating garment. And those ties, dangling down like a mockery of my modesty. As I laid down on the cold, hard table, I realised this was not just an ultrasound, this was something much more invasive, and I wasn't sure I could handle it. And then the doctor entered.

He was tall and imposing, with a sharpness in his eyes that made me want to shrink away. I couldn't even get a simple pap smear from my trusted GP without feeling uncomfortable, and now I had to endure this procedure with a stranger. My legs were awkwardly positioned in the stirrups, the cold metal making me flinch. The doctor started to explain the procedure, using words like 'dye' and 'cervical wall'. But all I could focus on was the fact that I'd be awake and he'd let me know if there was a blockage. My chest tightened and I felt like I couldn't breathe. I wished Jed were here, holding my hand and reassuring me. But I told him not to come, that I could handle it on my own. And now I regretted it. As the procedure began, the pain shot through my body. The doctor's words echoed in my mind as the dye was flushed through my tubes. *I can't believe I agreed to this. Where is the anaesthetic? Why did I think I could handle this alone?* I closed my eyes and tried to focus on my breathing, but it felt like I was drowning in fear and discomfort. This was not just another scan, this was a physical and emotional ordeal. And I was not prepared for it.

I'm still shocked to this day that the procedure is done

this way. I have a pretty good pain tolerance, but this was ridiculous. After flushing the pipes so to speak, I was given a preliminary all clear as nothing untoward was found. It was all done, another test down. They pulled me off the table and sent me to the cubicle where my things were waiting with a surfboard pad in tow. The nurse said I'd have some minor bleeding. *Really, you think?* I wanted to throttle her!

I left the clinic and waddled down the street with my surfboard in my underwear, completely perplexed at what had just happened. I called Jed and Mum and put on a brave face, but I was in agony. *Why didn't the GP give me more information on this? I should have asked more questions.*

As we settled back into our normal routine, the official results of the test came in and everything appeared to be in order. We breathed a sigh of relief, grateful for this victory and the absence of any issues. Let's make sure we never have to endure that test again! During this time, we continued to try conceiving naturally, putting the traumatic test behind us. And then, a few weeks later, my period was one day late. This was a major deviation from my regular, punctual cycle. *Could I possibly be pregnant without any medical intervention? Or perhaps it was the flushing pipes test that helped us conceive?* My mind raced with a million possibilities: each thought more anxiety-inducing than the last. I felt like I was losing my mind as I awaited the outcome.

Each day that passed, I tested for pregnancy, hoping for that elusive double line. I was so desperate for it that I scrutinised every little symptom hoping they were signs of a growing life inside of me. My breasts were sore, my stomach felt strangely warm, and I battled waves of nausea every morning. I knew these could all be attributed to other things, but I couldn't help but feel that they were all connected to my possible pregnancy. Call me crazy, but I just had this gut feeling. It was 3am on a Sunday morning when I finally couldn't take it anymore. I snuck out of bed and crept to the bathroom, my heart racing with nerves. I took another test, praying for those two lines to appear. And when they finally did, I felt a surge of emotion that I couldn't contain. I burst into our bedroom, shaking Jed awake and shoving the test in his face.

Poor guy, it took him a moment to comprehend what was happening, probably thinking we were being robbed or something. But as soon as it sunk in, his smile was the biggest I had ever seen. We were finally pregnant! It was a moment of pure joy, as we started to plan all the adventures that awaited us with our little baby. We had conceived naturally, and our whole world was filled with overwhelming happiness. I was only five weeks pregnant, but it already felt like a lifetime of love and excitement lay ahead of us. As I look back on that moment now, I can still feel the intensity of emotion that

NO FENCE, NO LIMITS

swept over me. It was a mix of fear, hope, and pure bliss. And at that moment, I knew our journey towards parenthood had truly begun.

The next morning was a blur of excitement and nervousness as I woke up knowing I was about to play soccer. I couldn't wipe the smile off my face, the anticipation building in my chest. But as I got dressed, doubts began to creep in. *Should I be playing? Would it be safe for the baby?* My mind raced as I debated whether I should call my friends and cancel. But then I remembered my closest friend Danielle had played soccer while pregnant with her second child. She had reassured me that it was safe and encouraged me to follow my passion. With her words in mind, I made the decision to go ahead with the game. I arrived at the field, my heart pounding with excitement and nerves. Dan gave me a congratulatory hug, her contagious smile only adding to my own. Now we both knew the feeling of being pregnant while playing soccer, and it brought us even closer. As the game began, I played full back, determined to give it my all. But as the second half rolled around, I couldn't ignore the pounding in my chest and the discomfort in my stomach. I had already been hit in the boobs multiple times, but the biggest blow was yet to come.

A ball hit me square in the stomach, and I felt something shift inside me. In a flash, I was off the field, tears streaming

36

down my face. Dan rushed over, her eyes filled with concern. She knew immediately that I was done for the day, and I felt like such an idiot. *What had I been thinking, putting my baby at risk like that?* I raced to the bathroom, my heart racing as I feared the worst. But Dan's mum, who had been watching the game, came to my rescue. She comforted me and reminded me that it was just the size of a peanut, nothing to worry about. And she was right, but it didn't stop the fear and anxiety from taking over. From that moment on, I knew I couldn't play soccer anymore.

As I rested that afternoon, cramps began to set in. My mind was consumed with worry, so I took another pregnancy test the next day. But to my surprise, there were no lines. *How could that be?* I had a positive test just the day before. I convinced myself that it must have been a faulty test, not wanting to worry Jed. As anyone who has struggled with fertility knows, the mind can play tricks on you. But deep down, I knew I was pregnant and everything would be okay. A week went by, and the cramps continued. People told me it was normal, that pregnancy can often feel like your period is coming but it never actually does. But I couldn't shake the feeling that something was wrong. After all, I had a positive pregnancy test. What could possibly be the problem?

We arrived at another weekend of soccer, and it was Mother's Day, the air heavy with the scent of freshly cut grass and the sound of cheering fans. I was buzzing with excitement, imagining all the future Mother's Days I would spend with our baby. I could almost feel the softness of newborn skin against mine and hear their sweet coos filling the air. But for now, I had decided to skip playing soccer and instead lent a hand at our local club's canteen. As the day went on, I couldn't shake the nagging cramps that seemed to intensify with each passing hour. Each stab of pain shot through me like a lightning bolt, making me fear the worst. I tried to hold it in, not wanting to face the possibility of what might be happening. But eventually, my bladder was screaming for release, and I had no choice but to make my way to the toilets. There, in the privacy of the stall, my heart sank as I saw the telltale brown stain.

Panic set in as I tried to come to terms with the possibility that I might be losing my baby. I had no idea what to do or what to expect, and the fear consumed me. Despite my fears, I tried to convince myself that everything was normal. That this happens to every pregnant woman. That it was just the baby growing and getting rid of old blood. I clung onto this hope, desperately trying to push away the thoughts of losing my baby. But by Wednesday, the brown stain had transformed into a bright red flow. The pain had become unbearable, and I knew I needed to seek help. At work, I could barely hold back the tears as I ran to my boss, blurting out that I had to leave.

I couldn't even explain what was happening, the words were stuck in my throat.

Desperate for answers, I called my GP and begged for an appointment. But they couldn't fit me in and I felt lost, not knowing where to turn or who to go to for help. All I wanted was someone to tell me what to do, to guide me through this terrifying experience. But at that moment, I was alone and scared, with no idea of what was to come.

The experience of miscarriage is one that is truly indescribable. It's a whirlwind of emotions, sensations, and pain that leaves you feeling completely empty and helpless. You can almost feel the weight of the baby you had hoped to carry full term slipping away, leaving a void in your heart and in your arms. And to make matters worse, this miscarriage was happening in the cold, sterile waiting room of a hospital. Since we couldn't get into my GP, we went to the local hospital. As we sat there, Jed and I felt like lifeless, forgotten souls, numb to the world around us. And as the pain intensified, we were left alone to endure the agony of loss. I could feel every ache and cramp, each one building upon the last until it reached a tipping point. It was like severe period pain, but there was no relief in sight. No amount of paracetamol or ibuprofen could dull the ache that seemed to consume my entire being.

I was hunched over in pain, desperate for someone to tell me that it was going to be okay. But no one came. We waited and waited in that hospital waiting room, the minutes feeling like an eternity. And then the pain reached its peak, and I could no longer hold on. I stumbled to the waiting room toilets, where we lost our baby at only 6 weeks. I left that cubicle feeling lifeless, watching as the 6-week-old sac was flushed away. And still, we waited. Waited for someone to tell us what to do, what was going to happen next.

Finally, a doctor saw me and took some bloods, then sent us home in the most clinical and detached way possible. I was terrified, mortified, and utterly alone. We were left to deal with the aftermath of our loss on our own. But the pain of that day will never leave me. The feeling of emptiness, the helplessness, the loss of a life that was just beginning. We were just a statistic to the hospital, another miscarriage case. But to us, it was our baby, our hopes and dreams, flushed away in a hospital toilet. And the only thing we were left with was the overwhelming feeling of being completely isolated.

✳ ✳ ✳

The following day, we sat in the bleak and sterile waiting room, the stench of disinfectant and sickness once again filling our nostrils. The harsh fluorescent lights seemed to intensify the heavy silence that hung in the air. I could feel my heart beating faster and faster, the anxiety building up inside me like a raging inferno. Beside me sat Jed, his face a mask of exhaustion and sorrow. I could tell he was trying to be strong for me, but I could see the cracks forming in his facade. I reached out and took his hand, seeking comfort in the simple touch.

The doctor finally arrived with a serious expression etched on his face. I couldn't help but think I would have preferred a female doctor at this moment, but I pushed the thought aside as he spoke. "Mrs Donougher, we're ready for you now."

My heart dropped at his words. I didn't want to face the truth, to confirm what we already knew. But I had to be strong, for myself and for Jed. As we entered the ultrasound room, I couldn't shake the feeling of dread that was settling in my stomach. I quickly changed into a hospital gown and lay down on the table, feeling exposed and vulnerable. The doctor began the scan, his movements slow and methodical. I could feel tears welling up in my eyes as I watched the screen, hoping against hope for a different outcome. But it was not meant to be. The doctor's grave expression said it all.

There was no baby. My heart shattered into a million pieces as I struggled to process the news. I looked over at Jed, and I could see the pain and devastation etched onto his face. He had been my rock through all of this, but I knew that he was hurting just as much as I was. But then, the doctor's words brought a new wave of fear crashing over me. He had noticed something on one of my ovaries, a small lump that could potentially be a cyst.

At that moment, I felt like my whole world was falling apart. I couldn't help but think, *why did this have to be so hard for us? Why did we have to endure so much pain and heartache?* It all seemed so unfair. But we had to pick ourselves up and carry on, as we always did. And as we left the hospital, I couldn't help but feel like a failure. Like I had failed to do the one thing that my body was supposed to do. But deep down, I knew that I was stronger than this. And with Jed by my side, I knew that we could get through anything that life threw our way.

* * *

I can still remember the sickening feeling in the pit of my stomach as I sat in the doctor's office, listening to her explain the results of the tests on the lump on my ovaries. Jed sat next to me, his hand clenched tightly around mine, his face a mask of worry and fear. I could feel tears stinging my eyes, threatening to spill at any moment. The doctor's words washed over me like a tidal wave, and I struggled to make sense of them.

An ovarian dermoid cyst filled with hair and teeth was growing inside my body. It made me want to gag just thinking about it. I couldn't even comprehend how something like that could exist inside me. As the doctor left the room, I felt like I had the most complicated and messed up body on the planet. I couldn't help but blame myself, wondering what I had done to deserve this. And in that moment, I felt like I had lost everything. But Jed was there, his grip on my hand never wavering. He was my rock, my constant, and I couldn't imagine going through this without him by my side.

Amid all this chaos, we attended the wedding of one of Jed's oldest friends in Queensland. We decided to still go despite everything that was happening. And as we arrived, I couldn't help but feel out of place, surrounded by happy couples and babies. And then it happened. I blurted out the news of my miscarriage to Jed's friends, as they stood there with their 5-month-old baby. I cringed at my own awkwardness, but our friends were nothing but understanding and supportive. They were our lifeline in that moment, and I will forever be grateful for their love and understanding. But the weekend was tough, as we watched our friends reach new milestones while we were left behind, our dreams shattered and our hearts aching.

When we returned home, I went to see the gynaecologist I had booked an appointment with when I first found out I was pregnant. And that's when she confirmed it – I had a cyst on my right ovary that needed to be removed. So, on top of everything else, I now had to undergo laparoscopic surgery to remove the cyst. I felt like I was being hit from all sides, each blow more painful than the last. But I knew I had to keep fighting, keep pushing forward. I couldn't let this defeat me. I had to keep going, for Jed, for myself, and for our future.

JED'S PERSPECTIVE

When Kelly first embarked on writing this book all those years ago, I was as supportive as I should be, but to be honest, I was hoping against hope that she would never ask me to contribute to it. I recognised that it would be a kind of therapy for her to let go of everything that we had been through. As the years rolled by, the book had always been on the agenda but not necessarily at the forefront of everything that Kelly was trying to achieve. Life is busy and prioritising the book came at the expense of so many other ideas that Kelly was trying to fit into our life and thankfully, have taken off.

But then it happened, and Kelly asked me to contribute. I did ask why, and her answer was that it would be great to get a male account on the fertility ride that never went the full circle for us.

"Are you kidding me?" I replied.

All sorts of things start running through my mind. *You want me, a red-blooded Australian male to put his feelings down on paper for whatever person that buys your book to read?* I'd be exposing some very raw feelings that I had buried well within my consciousness and put them out there to be critiqued by the public at their leisure. *No, no, no, I can't do that, period.*

The months and even years rolled by and I had some time to reassess my stance. I needed time to analyse things from every angle and came to the conclusion that I should contribute to it. Maybe I could make a difference to another man in a similar position who, like me, has trouble expressing or dealing with his emotions.

So here it goes.

There is no way around it, females bear children, and it is a rite of passage into womanhood for many. Should a woman wish to start a family and there are fertility issues, then it can be confronting for them to come to terms that they won't get what they have longed for. Yes, you can start the IVF process and hopefully the end result is one that brings joy and celebration, but what they don't tell you is that there is a percentage of couples who will not achieve this. It's a bit like participating in the lottery – you hope against hope of winning it but there is a very real chance that you won't. Kelly was one of those women who thought this was a given for her and more importantly, us.

While we were going through all of this, my siblings were starting their own families and we have nephews and nieces that we adore so much, but at the time, while I was always positive with the news another pregnancy was confirmed, I just wished that it was us. Being an extremely tight family unit, I know my siblings were always conscious of telling us their fantastic news and it was another knock-on effect of infertility that it was now affecting them as well. They should have been able to share their news without continually weighing up whether to tell us or not for fear of upsetting us. This is something else I couldn't control or remedy. The downward spiral continued. The longer this continued, the more I felt numb, indifferent, confused and above all, heartbroken.

Everyone has a life story that is made up of the good, the bad and the ugly. While everyone's story is different, part of my story is on the back of a failed first marriage that also had fertility issues. While infertility comes in different forms, the same sorts of feelings are present all the way through so I wasn't totally new to this and felt I may have had some grounding in how to handle all of this, wherever this led us. I was lucky enough to have a daughter from my first so I thought *why wouldn't we end up with the same result?*

SWIMMING THROUGH THE DENIAL

After the initial shock wears off, denial can take its place. This stage is marked by the reinforcement of a mental fence, one that keeps out unwanted thoughts while tightly guarding the version of life we're still trying to salvage. Denial becomes a strange kind of hope, one that is sharp-edged, exhausting and unsustainable.

If you're in denial, know that it's okay if you feel:

- Like you're clinging to hope with white knuckles

- Exhausted from trying to control the uncontrollable

- Afraid to consider alternatives because they feel like giving up

- Triggered by other people's success, especially when they mirror what you want

- Obsessed with finding a loophole, solution, or exception to the rule

- Disconnected from your own intuition

Denial can take two forms. The first is the denial that this is the final chapter, a quiet insistence that the plan is still intact, just... delayed. It can look like hyper-commitment and determination. You double down, dig in, and convince yourself that if you just work harder, be more positive, follow all the right steps, things will fall back into place. The dream isn't dead, you tell yourself. It just needs more time or a different approach. We reinforce the path with effort, optimism, and stories that validate our persistence. We want to hear about the woman who got miraculously pregnant after seven years of trying, the person whose conservative parents came around and accepted them for being trans, or the hopeful NBA player who gets drafted after years of failure. It all fuels this belief that the setbacks are just that – setbacks on a road that eventually leads to success.

This is the kind of denial that presented for me, as I experienced a renewed push to *make* it happen. I shifted from feeling sad and confused about not being able to conceive after those few months into solutions mode. I focused on everything that I had control over and identified all the ways I could contribute positively to the desired outcome. Even after the miscarriage, I refused to believe that meant it was never going to happen. We were going to conceive, so what did I need to do to make this happen? As much pain as we'd endured so far, deep in my soul I needed to believe that I was going to fall pregnant and that we would have the family we'd so desperately wanted.

On the other hand, denial can be a sense of disbelief or a refusal to acknowledge the situation for what it really is. This is more common for the expectations that you know deep down are not right for you, but you're soldiering on because something or someone else is telling you it's what you *should* do. If this is you, then it could be time to stop and reflect honestly with yourself. Are you ignoring how you really feel because it contradicts what you've been told to believe? What would it mean to you if it didn't happen the way it's been planned? What are you pretending to not know?

CHAPTER 4

IS THE DEVIL AVAILABLE FOR A BARGAIN? ASKING FOR A FRIEND...

Bargaining is pretending
we still have leverage
with a universe that's
already said no.

he GP referred us to one of the top IVF clinics in Sydney, which left us with a glimmer of hope. But as we walked into the dark room to meet the doctor, I couldn't shake off the uneasy feeling in my stomach. His first question, delivered with a cold, matter-of-fact tone, hit me like a slap in the face. "Why have you come to me after only trying for 6 months?" I wanted to scream, "Six months is freaking ages and I don't have time to waste! I'm 25 now! And I've had a miscarriage." But instead, I just sat there, feeling small and insignificant. The barrage of tests that followed felt like a violation. Blood drawn, sperm tested, all in the name of finding out what was wrong with us. As we left the clinic, drained and silent, I couldn't help but feel a wave of fear wash over me. *What if there was something wrong with me?*

But as the results came back, everything seemed normal. My cyst was removed, and my abnormal pap smear was under control. We were given the green light to start with the less invasive option of intrauterine insemination (IUI). It involves inserting the sperm at the perfect moment, hoping for fertilisation to occur. The experts assured us that it was our best chance at success. But as we went through the process, I couldn't help but feel like we were just numbers, another couple going through the motions. There was no personal connection, no warmth or empathy from the doctors and nurses. Just a cold, clinical approach to something that was so deeply personal and emotional for us. Yet, we soldiered on, clinging onto the hope that this would be the answer to our prayers. We were determined to do whatever it took to become parents, even if it meant sacrificing our own well-being. And so we continued on, with a heavy heart and a growing sense of desperation.

While less intense than IVF, this process still comes with a barrage of testing, gruelling scans and hormone treatment that left my body feeling like a science experiment. Day after day, I was poked and prodded, my hormones manipulated to reach the perfect level for fertilisation. As if trying to lead a normal life and work a full-time job wasn't challenging enough, I also had to be available for testing at the exact right moments. This often meant sacrificing my personal life and sleep to rush to the hospital before work, enduring uncomfortable procedures, and then structuring my entire day around when the next test needed to be completed.

After enduring the first round of IUI with this clinic, we were met with crushing disappointment when we received the news that my eggs weren't viable for retrieval. I just didn't have enough. The excruciating wait for the call, the sinking feeling in my gut as I heard the words, it was all too much to bear. But still, we held onto hope and decided to dive straight into round two. Round two was a whole new level of intensity. The cramping was unbearable, but I had no idea what was causing it. It was my birthday, and instead of celebrating, I mustered up the courage to mention the pain to the doctors, and they proceeded with a transvaginal scan. That's when they discovered the reason for my suffering – too many eggs. *Too many eggs? How could this be?* One minute I didn't have enough and now I had too many? My heart shattered into a million pieces. But I soon learned the harsh reality of this type of IVF – it's a risky business. The threat of overstimulating the ovaries is a risk that hospitals and clinics simply won't take. And so, my cycle was abruptly terminated on the spot. I left the clinic feeling shattered, on my birthday of all days, and had to drag myself to work to pretend it was just another ordinary day. But deep down, I knew it was anything but ordinary.

✳ ✳ ✳

A year into our fertility struggles, my hairdresser shared with me her excitement about a new IVF clinic. As a gay woman, she and her partner were beginning the journey of starting a family. She raved about the clinic, praising its incredible doctor and welcoming environment that felt more personal. I no longer wanted to be just another number in a hospital waiting room. I wanted to feel like my journey was important and that someone was truly listening to me. Something felt off and I needed answers. I longed for someone to show us they cared.

Our first meeting with the doctor was a refreshing change from the sterile hospital settings we had grown accustomed to. Her practice was in a converted historical home, exuding luxury and charm. As we sat in the beautifully decorated rooms with ornate details and stunning artwork, I couldn't help but appreciate the doctor's vision of creating a welcoming and familial atmosphere for her clients. Looking back, I realise that my interior design instincts were already stirring. I was drawn to the old bones of the home and the rich, dark floors.

During the meeting, Jed seemed to feel uncomfortably scrutinised. As a former football player with a muscular build, he felt like the doctor's questions were presumptuous and probing. It was as if she was trying to uncover if he had ever used steroids during his playing days. He left the clinic with a bitter taste in his mouth, feeling judged and rightfully so, as the questions were completely unfounded and unnecessary.

As the meeting ended, the doctor's voice became more confident and assured. "I can't see any reason why you won't be pregnant within the year," she declared boldly. My heart soared with hope, trusting in her expertise and years of experience. My husband was more sceptical, trying to temper my excitement. But I was determined to focus on the positives, feeding him reassurance and optimism. Little did I realise, my husband was struggling more than I could ever imagine during this journey. It was easy to forget that he was also going through a great deal of pain and despair, even though it was my body enduring the physical toll. Mentally, the weight on his shoulders was just as heavy.

With newfound determination and a new clinic, we embarked on our second attempt of IVF, full of hope and promise. This time, we opted for a more advanced approach: intracytoplasmic sperm injection (ICSI). It was the recommended path for the highest chance of success. To our delight, we had five eggs retrieved in the first cycle. It felt like a huge win, and we were filled with optimism for this new journey and clinic. However, the egg retrieval process was more painful than I had expected. The anxiety of going under general anaesthetic and waking up to see a number on my hand indicating how many eggs were retrieved was nerve-wracking. The fear of something going wrong was always present, despite being closely monitored leading up to the procedure. In addition, we decided to have Jed's sperm extracted through a needle and syringe from his testes. It was a painful procedure, but we were willing to do whatever it took to get the best sperm. Plus, this method allowed us to freeze any additional sperm for future fertilisation attempts. We continued to closely monitor the eggs after fertilisation, but unfortunately, none were viable. It was back to the drawing board, with another round of blood tests and cycle testing. Through all of this, we refused to give up hope.

Meanwhile, the hormones coursed through my body, amplifying every emotion and sensation. I could feel the anxiety and desperation building up as we embarked on our second round with this clinic. The constant tests, the never-ending commute, the juggling of work and appointments – it was all taking its toll. And to make matters worse, we were in Sydney, where the traffic was a nightmare in itself. But we were determined to make this work. I had become accustomed to the onslaught of needles and injections, the pain and discomfort almost a routine now. Yet, amid all the chaos, we held onto hope. This cycle, we had two viable eggs. Two chances at finally becoming parents. We eagerly decided to implant both, the thought of having twins both exhilarating and daunting. But as any couple going through this journey knows, the wait after implantation is excruciating. Two weeks of uncertainty, of over-analysing every little change in my body, hoping and praying for a positive outcome.

This time, we had come closer than ever before. We had moved into a bigger house, with more bedrooms ready to welcome a family. I had even taken leave from work to be home when the call came in. And then, my phone rang. The news was devastating – I wasn't pregnant. Again. I couldn't hold back the tears any longer, and as the tradesmen worked on the roof, I retreated to the laundry to sob in solitude. I knew I couldn't continue like this, pretending that everything was fine when it wasn't. But I had to. I wiped away my tears, put on a brave face, and saw the tradesmen out. But as soon as they were gone, I collapsed onto the floor once again, the weight of disappointment and despair crushing me. *How was I going to tell Jed? Should I call him?* He was probably waiting for my call, anxiously hoping for good news. But I couldn't bring myself to do it. The rest of the day passed in a blur, the memories hazy and indistinct. All I knew was that my heart was breaking, and I didn't know how to fix it.

We pushed onwards though and started the third round of ICSI, determined to make our dream of having a baby a reality. I was really trying to enforce a positive environment on every round of fertility treatments. I'd wish and hope each round to convince myself that this one would be successful. I'd bargain with myself, thinking that if it was successful this time, then I promise I won't play sport, or I'll finish work early for maternity leave, or I'll rest more to keep the baby growing safely. I would have promised anything if I could just live out this dream of starting a family. It's funny looking back and realising that in the depths of despair, you'll tell yourself anything and it almost sounds like you're losing your mind, but it seems so plausible at the time.

The familiar routine of injections, appointments, and hopeful waiting consumed our lives once again. But this time, we vowed to ourselves that it would be different. We would not let disappointment or doubt creep in. We would keep pushing forward, no matter what. And so, we found ourselves back on the cycle again. The anticipation and anxiety built with each passing day, until finally, it was time for the embryo transfer. We held onto each other tightly, our hearts beating in unison as we placed all our hopes and dreams into that one tiny embryo. But the waiting game was far from over. We had to endure yet another two-week wait, filled with restless nights and constant thoughts of what could be. And to add to the already intense situation, I was in the middle of peak summer season at work. As the director of all the swimming programs, my days were consumed by the chaos of the summer rush. And yet, my mind kept wandering back to the phone call that would change our lives forever.

Finally, the day arrived. The call that would determine our future came at 2:30pm. My heart was pounding so loudly that I could barely hear the phone ring. With trembling hands, I answered and held my breath as the words spilled out: "Mrs. Donougher, we have your results. You're pregnant." The sheer elation that filled my heart was overwhelming. I could hardly believe it. After all the heartbreak and struggles, we were going to be parents. But as my mind raced with excitement, I knew I had to share this moment with my husband. I fumbled through my old Nokia phone, scrolling through the contacts until I found Jed's number. (Side note: How did we ever function with these archaic devices?) I dialled his number and waited, my heart bursting with anticipation. And then, finally, I heard his voice. "Babe, you're going to be a dad," I blurted out, barely able to contain my emotions. I had rehearsed this moment a million times in my head, but nothing could have prepared me for the overwhelming joy and love that filled Jed's voice. For years, we had silently shared the pain and heartache of our struggles to conceive. But in that moment, all of that was washed away by the pure happiness and hope that filled our hearts. We were going to be parents. And our journey, though filled with ups and downs, had brought us to this moment. A moment that we would cherish forever. A moment that would shape our lives in ways we could never have imagined.

The following weeks were a whirlwind of emotions, a rollercoaster ride of hope and fear. The anticipation of our first ultrasound was almost unbearable, but it gave us a sense of excitement and joy that we had not felt in a long time. We couldn't wait to share the news with our loved ones, to see the look of happiness on their faces. But amid all the happiness, there was still a lingering sense of unease. The memory of our previous loss was fresh in our minds, and it cast a shadow over our joy. Yet, we pushed those thoughts aside and basked in the joy of the moment, dreaming of the future and all the possibilities it held. As the day of the ultrasound approached, I couldn't shake off the anxiety that had been gnawing at me.

And then, it happened. The cramping began, and with it, a sinking feeling in my stomach. I desperately hoped that it was nothing, that it was just my nerves playing tricks on me. But as we sat in the waiting room, admiring the beautiful interiors of the clinic, I knew deep down that something was wrong. The cramping had intensified, and I feared the worst. I couldn't bring myself to say the words out loud to Jed, afraid that it would make it all too real. And then, the scan. The moment of truth. The nurses' faces said it all. Our worst nightmare was confirmed – the sack was empty and a miscarriage was inevitable. I felt like I had been punched in the gut, the pain and heartbreak overwhelming.

The nurses took some blood samples and sent us on our way, no follow-up with the doctor or any information on what to do next. Once again, it was like we were just another number to them, another statistic. I looked around the waiting room at all the hopeful couples waiting for their turn, and I couldn't help but feel a sense of isolation. We were alone in our grief, with no one to turn to. I couldn't process what was happening. I couldn't find the words to express the pain and devastation that consumed me. And the response from the nurses – "We will take some blood to assess your levels" – felt like a cold, impersonal dismissal of our pain. We all knew what was going to happen, yet no one stopped to ask us how we were feeling or offer any comfort. As we left the clinic that day, I couldn't help but feel like I had failed. Failed as a woman, as a wife, as a mother. And in that moment, I wished I had asked more questions, demanded more answers. But it was too late. The darkness of grief had already enveloped me, and I could see no way out.

The night was never-ending, the pain unbearable. I paced back and forth in the hallway, my hands clutching at my stomach as if I could somehow ease the agony. Every step felt like a knife being twisted in my gut. This miscarriage was far worse than the last one. I felt like I was being torn apart from the inside out, like I was going to black out at any moment. *Why did they send me home? Why wasn't I in the hospital? Why didn't they tell me what to do?* My mind was racing, my body screaming for relief. I wanted someone to just wrap me up and tell me it was going to be okay, but I was alone in my suffering. When the pain reached its peak, I could no longer stand. I stumbled to the bathroom and collapsed on the toilet, waiting for the inevitable to pass. Hours went by, and there it sat in the bottom of the toilet, a cruel reminder of what I had lost. Jed woke to the sound of my sobs and held me as I cried. Once again, he was my rock, my only source of comfort.

The next day, I mustered up the strength to speak with the doctor, but it proved to be a difficult task. At no point did I feel supported or consoled. The response was cold and clinical, asking when I wanted to book in for another round of treatment. In that moment, I was filled with anger and resentment. *How could they be so callous? How could they not see the pain I was in?* "Go fuck yourself," I wanted to scream, but instead, I just walked away.

I've always been known for my drive and ambition, for my determination to succeed no matter the cost. But in this instance, that drive was a curse. I often put my work before myself or even my marriage, something I'm still struggling to find balance with to this day. In fact, just days after this miscarriage, I was due to represent my workplace in a local government management challenge. Despite the physical and emotional toll, I pushed myself to compete and we placed third. Looking back, I know that the mental distraction was necessary, but deep down, I also know that I needed time to grieve and heal.

JED'S PERSPECTIVE

I am under no illusion that women take the brunt of most fertility issues. A man is pretty much limited to sperm collection, donor sperm from an outside source, freezing sperm, or a combination of all. And when those options don't contribute to the solution, there can be feelings of guilt that there's nothing else they can do and the woman has to bear the rest of the burden.

I know that any fertility clinic would beg to differ, but like all businesses, they are primarily there to make money whether it be for themselves or stakeholders in the company. I have no doubt that some clinics leverage the fact that you are so emotionally involved in having a child that you forget, most times, why you were in a partnership in the first place.

Over the course of so many clinics and cycles, as a man and partner it was very hard to watch someone you love go through something that, in my mind, should be as natural as riding a bike. I feel I was underprepared and ill-informed in part for what was to be a 'normal' life for us in the foreseeable future. The injections, the blood tests, the preparation for egg collecting, the sterile and most times inhospitable clinic rooms aren't fully explained in any detail. It was primarily a case that I expected to have my head in the sand and when I brought my head out of it, all will be as it should be. Maybe the process was fully explained to me at the time, but Kelly understood what was happening every step of the way and I was either too blasé or never fully comprehended the significance of it all.

I watched Kelly, the woman I truly adored and loved, take hit after hit after hit. From the disappointment of the clinic receptionist telling her the cycle had failed again to the mind and body altering chemical injections that changed Kelly's persona. These were the easier of the disappointments, the ones that got to me the most were the miscarriages. It was if we were able to start a new life, only for it to dissipate like it never happened. I won't lie, it was hard to watch, but the biggest struggle to all of this was not being able to do anything to help. How can a man fully comprehend what that is like? You can't, it's impossible and there is sure as hell no manual to read on how to deal with it.

Of course, there are now a plethora of groups and agencies that can help you deal with your emotions, depression and the like, which is great, but for my generation (X/Y), this is something you always dealt with yourself as if they don't exist. "I don't need help, I've got this."

The longer this journey progressed, I just couldn't find anyone to ask why it was us that couldn't have kids! Yes, we found out years later why and I now have a calmness about it all, but I'm still searching for the person to tell me why it had to be us. Are they out there at all? At the time, I searched high and low, but I sure as hell couldn't find them and this was by no means through a lack of trying!

LEAVING THE DEAL ON THE TABLE

Denial and bargaining can look very similar at first glance; however, where bargaining is different is that in this stage, you acknowledge that failure is a possibility, but you try everything you can to make it happen anyway. It's as if you're rowing on a river with a strong current that's pulling you towards the left path and you can see there's a real chance you'll go down it, but you row your absolute hardest to go right anyway.

This can involve searching for loopholes, alternative paths or compromises to achieve your outcome. For me, this was accepting that we might need medical intervention to conceive and trying multiple different procedures and methods to achieve pregnancy. I grappled with the idea that it might not ever happen, but that didn't mean I was ready to give up. In fact, it made me want to work for it even more. I would've made a deal with the devil if it meant I could've given birth to a healthy baby.

When you're in the bargaining stage, it's okay if you feel:

- Like you're willing to trade anything – time, comfort, even parts of yourself – for a different ending

- Like you're living two lives: one you show others, and one you secretly hope will still work out

- Exhausted from the mental math of constantly trying to make it work

- Tempted to ignore your own limits, boundaries, or truth to avoid disappointment or judgement

- Frightened by the idea that no matter what you give, it still might not be enough

When you're in this desperate, bargaining stage, you need to consider everything you're giving to make it happen and analyse whether it's viable. Is the path you're trying so hard to go down serving you or slowly eroding parts of who you are? Are you being honest about the costs of the bargain you're making? When we make these kinds of bargains with ourselves, what often happens is that the elements of ourselves that we've sacrificed in our compromise eventually resurface and we're forced to deal with them. It's like all those fantasy shows where the sorcerer reminds the protagonist that "All magic has a price." We might be fine to agree to that price in our bargaining stage, but it must be paid eventually.

If you're ready to move out of the bargaining stage and towards healing and acceptance, it can be helpful to write down everything you're trading or compromising to hold onto your expected outcome and ask yourself if you're being fair to yourself. Consider putting some boundaries into place that you might have been ignoring and create a list of non-negotiables that you need to protect your health.

CHAPTER 5

DEPRESSION IS OFTEN THE PRICE

When the truth stops negotiating, all that's left is the ache of what never arrived.

The last 6 years had been a relentless storm, battering us from all sides. It was a storm of loss and disappointment, of endless tests and treatments, of shattered hopes and crushed dreams. We were drained and exhausted mentally and physically, mere shells of our former selves. Two miscarriages. Countless tests. Two IVF clinics. Three IUI cycles. Three ICSI cycles.

It seemed like the universe was conspiring against us, throwing one obstacle after another in our path. And we were left to pick up the pieces, again and again. I was at my breaking point. My body, once a source of pride and strength, was now a source of disgust and shame. I couldn't bear to look at myself in the mirror, let alone face the world. Everywhere I turned, there was sadness and pity. My relationship with my mother had soured, weighed down by unspoken grief.

But it wasn't just the external world that was suffocating me. It was my own mind. The constant barrage of questions and doubts, the fear of never becoming a mother, the guilt of feeling jealous of those who were. It was suffocating, consuming me from the inside out. Even Jed couldn't save me from myself. I could see the worry in his eyes, the fear that one day I might just shatter into a million pieces and never be put back together. And I couldn't blame him. I was starting to hate myself, everything about me. Life had become an endless cycle of irritations and frustrations.

Jed and I knew we couldn't keep going like this, subjecting ourselves to endless rounds of treatments, only to be met with disappointment. My body was done, and so was I. Jed, ever the supportive husband, went along with my decision. But deep down, I couldn't help but wonder if he had wanted to keep trying, if he had given up on our dream of having a family. But it didn't matter anymore. The signs were there, looming over us like dark clouds. I was losing myself, and I wasn't sure if I could find my way back.

The weight of our unfulfilled dream of parenthood was crushing. I couldn't bear to see the disappointment and heartache in my parents' eyes as they watched us go through endless treatments and still not conceive. It was a constant reminder of our failure, and it took a toll on our relationship. We were no longer the close mother and daughter we used to be. Our once cherished conversations turned into strained silences, and I couldn't help but wonder if things would ever be the same again.

It's easy in these moments of stress, anxiety and disappointment to fall into the trap of constant comparison. I honestly believe we are all our own worst enemy when the comparison and unrealistic expectations take hold and it's all you can see. We are in a world of so much noise thanks to social media and the way we pressure ourselves to be better than what we see while we scroll through our feeds. We are surrounded by the belief that the next person has it better than us – a better life, better family, better job… the list goes on. In these moments of despair, all I could do was compare. I was brought up to believe that my life had to follow a particular path, and I wasn't on it.

As much as I tried to stay strong and positive, there were moments when I felt like I was losing myself. The constant pressure and disappointment were taking a toll on my mental and emotional well-being. I found myself retreating into a protective shell, shutting out those who tried to push me to keep trying. I threw myself into work and other projects, trying to distract myself from the all-consuming world of infertility. But in doing so, I also shut out my loved ones, including my own mother, who didn't understand my coping mechanism.

It wasn't until after Jed's 40th birthday when my parents offered us money to continue with IVF that I realised how strained our relationship had become. I knew they were just trying to help, but at that point, I didn't want anything. I was at my breaking point, feeling like a failure and hating myself for not being able to fulfill the one thing I had always wanted. I just wanted someone to tell me it was going to be okay. But as much as I longed for my mother's comforting words, I also understood that she came from a different generation with different perspectives and ways of coping. Amid all the pain and struggles, I couldn't see it. But now, I can finally empathise with her and the strain our shared dream had put on our relationship.

This period of our life was by far the most traumatising and exhausting, filled with a rollercoaster of emotions. I knew I wasn't alone but at the same time I felt more alone than ever in this journey to become parents. If you are on a similar path now, I see you, I know the anguish, the all-consuming gut-wrenching feeling, the exhaustion of keeping up with society's view on what your life should look like and the constant comparison. I want you to know that you are not alone. I know you're not ready to accept, embrace and move past grief and that's okay. I encourage you to find that person in your life you can confide in and lean on. My hope for you is that you find that one soul who listens and doesn't need to talk, the person who doesn't need to fill the air with their thoughts on what you should do or what they think will help. A person who just listens.

I learnt a lot and discovered a lot and created some long lasting friendships that really helped me through the dark times. Never underestimate the power of a real friendship. The ones who just listen when you need to and can pick up the phone and chat like it was yesterday even though you haven't spoken in weeks.

JED'S PERSPECTIVE

There are a few moments in life where things are beyond our control. Death, taxes and of course, infertility. I felt helpless and anyone who has felt this way knows it to be one of the worst feelings in the world where any light at the end of the tunnel seems so far away. Unreachable even. Having said this, I had to remain strong and positive for Kelly. After all, we're in this together, but how do I do this when I am doubting my own ability to not only look after myself but Kelly as well?

Did I properly deal with the disappointment of it all? No, I didn't. I look back now and while I think I portrayed the ever-supportive husband and did, I hope, say and do the right things for Kelly, inside I was at the lowest ebb of my life. Gutted! A void deepened the further we travelled on this journey, with the ever-present realisation that this journey wasn't going to end at a destination that would bring tears of joy for us rather than gut-wrenching hurt.

Having been through what we had and the emotions, which I now realise sent me into depression, it's clear to me that people shouldn't do this alone, no matter how well you think you are coping with it. Without doubt, everyone has a breaking point because we are all human after all, and it goes with the old adage: "A problem shared is a problem halved." Yes, be as supportive as you can for your partner, let them vent, cry, smash walls or whatever, but don't lose track of the fact that the support person also needs help sometimes. I feel this is lost in the world sometimes. Don't lose sight of yourself.

* * *

We continued our robotic existence in Sydney. Eat, sleep, repeat! Clinic after clinic, test after test and disappointment after disappointment. The strain of it all was starting to take effect and while I never thought our relationship was in danger of failing, we definitely weren't the couple we were two years prior. We were both in highly stressful jobs, driving continually in Sydney peak hour traffic, trying to conceive a child with everything associated with that and all the while trying to maintain a positive outlook to family and friends who all said, "It'll happen eventually."

My immediate family is one that you could only wish for. Being a little biased, I have parents and siblings that I know I was blessed to be a part of their lives and would totally argue that they are the best in the world. They were supportive, understanding and all in all, they are my best friends outside of Kelly. They did what they all thought was right in the advice given, but in the back of my mind, this wasn't going to end in the result we were all hoping for.

Then, the fork in the road moment happened. We had friends in Queensland, and I was due to head to Brisbane to oversee a couple of jobs that had started and was booked to stay for two weeks in the town centre. By chance, a phone call from our friend who knew I was in the area asked to meet up for dinner and the date was cemented. The dinner was like any other you have with friends. We laughed, reminisced, ate way too much and then a question was asked of me that took me a little off guard. "Would you and Kelly move to WA to work in a mine that we are going to be working at?" I sat there and absorbed the information and the next words out of my mouth were, "Yes, but I don't think Kelly would!"

I ended up ringing Kelly that night and told her about the conversation I'd had, and she wasn't totally against the idea. When I returned to Sydney, we both had time to digest the information and sat down and did a pro/con list. The evidence heavily favoured going to WA. There were a multitude of reasons to leave our life in Sydney and start fresh elsewhere; however, it was going to be a gamble that could backfire and leave us without a house or jobs. We planned to only go for three years, which we thought would be plenty of time to distract us from fertility issues and hopefully make some good money to explore a part of Australia that neither of us had really been to.

MANAGING THE DEPRESSION

There comes a moment when the weight of it all just lands. The bargaining has been exhausted, the effort has run dry, and there's nothing left to push against. What follows isn't always loud or visible. It can feel like a low fog settling in. This is the depression stage: not just sadness, but a deep, aching grief for the life you expected to live and the version of you who was supposed to live it.

This stage carries a kind of emotional exhaustion that's hard to explain to others. You may find yourself questioning everything: *Who am I without this goal? What do I want now?* There's a hollowing-out that happens here, and with it can come a sense of identity loss that's more than emotional – it's existential.

You might find that your energy disappears. Even small tasks feel monumental. You might want to withdraw, or you might go through the motions while feeling totally disconnected from your life. This is normal. You're not lazy or broken – your mind and body are reacting to prolonged uncertainty, unmet expectations, and the slow unravelling of a future you once believed was certain.

Managing this stage isn't about fixing it, it's about tending to it. Giving yourself permission to feel without rushing to reframe it as a lesson or a blessing. Allowing the grief to pass through you without trying to outthink it. You're not weak for feeling this way. You're human and this is what it looks like when a story ends before the next one has fully formed.

When you're going through this period of depression, know that it's okay if you feel:

- Like the world is continuing without you and you're stuck in place

- Emotionally numb or detached from things you used to care about

- Exhausted by the weight of unprocessed grief and prolonged uncertainty

- Confused about who you are without the goal you've let go of

- Afraid that joy or hope won't return

CHAPTER 6

EXPERIMENTING WITH NEW VERSIONS OF THE SCRIPT

When the door you
want disappears,
look for the keys
to other ones.

*D*uring this period, Tanya became my salvation. She was my personal trainer, and her contagious optimism was exactly what I needed in my life at this point. I have no doubt that our meeting was no coincidence. She is a dear and enduring friend, with a heart of gold and a great sense of humour. Even during the most challenging time of her second baby's birth, she never let on that she was struggling or sleep deprived. I put in a lot of effort at her personal training studio and lost 10 kilograms. I was smashing my goals and feeling fantastic, but the pain of our struggles lingered.

One day, Tanya suggested that I visit her friend Betty, a spiritual woman who had helped Tanya's family through various illnesses and provided guidance. At that point, I was willing to try anything non-medical to improve my situation. Little did I know that this would be the beginning of my heightened awareness of the world and people around me. However, in all my searching, I had overlooked one important person: Jed. Our relationship had reached its breaking point, mentally, physically, and emotionally. Meeting Betty was a pivotal moment both for me and for us.

During our first encounter, I felt a weight lift off my shoulders in Betty's calming presence and she spoke with such wisdom and grace. She was inspiring, uplifting, and had a spiritual aura that is difficult to put into words. Betty was an 'old soul' with a deep understanding of the world, and there was something undeniably special about her. During our consultations, Betty mentioned that she could see a big change coming for Jed and me. We were considering moving to Perth, and Betty encouraged us to go for it. She even had a vision of our future home, perched high on a hill with a breathtaking view of the ocean. At the time, I brushed it off as a dream, but little did I know that it would become a reality in the years to come.

Looking back, I realise that meeting Betty was meant to be. Her words and guidance have stayed with me throughout the years. Her wisdom and intuition were a gift, and I often find myself reflecting on our conversations and how they've shaped our lives. It was like the universe was guiding us towards our next journey in life. And as we took that leap of faith and moved to Perth, we discovered that Betty was right. It was the beginning of a new and exciting chapter in our lives, one that we never could have imagined without her guidance. It's amazing how putting our desires out into the universe can lead to such incredible and unexpected outcomes. I will always be grateful for her presence and the role she played in kick-starting the next chapter of our journey together.

Moving to Perth was no light decision, as our entire lives were in Sydney. Our families, my stepdaughter, all our friends and the security of our home and jobs that we'd been in for 20 years combined. Broaching the subject with my family was like walking on hot coals. Our parents, from completely different generations, could not comprehend the idea of uprooting our lives and moving to a new place. For my mum, it was utterly incomprehensible. The thought of leaving the safety and familiarity of everything we knew was terrifying to her. But we had to do it, as we knew it was our only choice if we wanted to survive.

My mum and I are very different personalities, and I now understand each of our triggers more and I am more understanding of the fact that she sees change very differently to me. Change is something that is not foreign or scary to me, and I thrive off the experience and embrace every facet of it. But this is certainly not something I was brought up with. It has taken me many years to understand change, the way it can make you feel and the uncertainty it can bring. I've had to push through the trauma and those beliefs that change was a negative thing and that your environment had to stay the same to move forward or because that's what everyone else did. I believe that everyone has the power to make change and you have the power to make a difference to your life if you want it.

Leaving Sydney taught us many things, but it also repaired many wounds too and I know my mum now sees that moving to Perth was something we had to do. We had dealt with so much adversity, shock, denial, depression, guilt and were trying to let go of expectations. I don't think we ever really discussed the IVF chapter being closed permanently, but we knew we needed a change, and we needed a life that wasn't about having children, careers or a new home. It was about moving forward, as this was the only option. It's the only thing I know how to do. It was honestly a relief to just let go.

So, in 2012, we packed up our entire life in just two weeks – house, car, and all belongings – and headed to Perth without a home lined up yet. It was one of the scariest decisions we had ever made, but it was time for a change. And with that change came a newfound sense of freedom.

We were no longer confined by the expectations and routines of our previous lives. We were free to explore, to take risks, and to follow our intuition. This period marked a complete reset in our lives. Leaving the past behind, we aimed to reshape our future and rediscover joy. The expectation of what we thought our life was supposed to look like was slowly dissolving and we were creating a new chapter. One that we never thought possible. While my family still wasn't a keen advocate for us moving, there was no looking back for us. We had moved away from everyone else's white picket fence story and started creating a version of our own.

Our move to Perth was accompanied by an incredible opportunity on a mine site – yes, mining! The hi-vis clothing, steel cap boots, flies and red dirt that creeps into every crevice of your clothing, hair and skin was far from anything I'd ever known or expected to know. A far cry from my 9–5 days in high heels, local government and the fitness swimming industry, mining gave me a new challenge and one that I desperately needed. I'd found a place that was exactly where I needed to be at that time. The mining world is one that is truly hard to describe until you've experienced it. It's a community where you live, work, eat, repeat with the same group of people 14–16 hours a day for up to 2 weeks at a time depending on your roster. They became like family. As weird as it sounds, our mining career and family came to us exactly when we needed it. Now when I walked into a room, the question wasn't if I have children, it was what my role in mining was. I was seen as something else other than a woman born to get married and bear children.

This path had opened a door to something else that we hadn't expected. We were meeting new people, going on adventures, and creating a life we didn't know we could have. Mining was challenging me in a whole new way. I was bringing skills and resilience from my previous life into a new format, and I was proud. I was working through the ranks and being recognised for achieving amazing things for the company. I was becoming a new person with different goals and visions and passions that I didn't even realise existed. There were no expectations

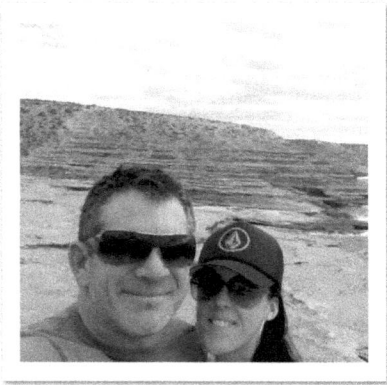

in mining either; we were all treated equally and had the same goal. I met some truly remarkable people in my mining time, ones that came to me exactly when I needed them. There was no history with them or pre-conceived ideas on how I should look as a female in my 30s, and I'm forever grateful for those friendships.

As we settled into our new life in Western Australia, we couldn't help but feel a sense of peace and contentment. The warm sun, gentle ocean breeze, and stunning natural beauty enveloped us in the hug we so desperately needed. Despite the challenges we faced with IVF, we were grateful to have found a place that truly felt like home. Our days were no longer filled with stress and worry, but instead, they were spent soaking up the laid-back lifestyle that Perth had to offer. We traded in our busy schedules for lazy days spent lounging on the beach, watching the crystal clear waters lap against the shore. And with each passing day, we found ourselves falling more and more in love with this new way of life. But it wasn't just the idyllic surroundings that brought us joy. It was the people we met and the connections we made along the way. The sense of community in Perth was unlike anything we had experienced before. We were welcomed with open arms and quickly made new friends who became like family to us. It was in this new environment, among supportive and caring individuals, that we found ourselves truly thriving. Our minds were clear, our hearts were full, and our outlook on life was forever changed.

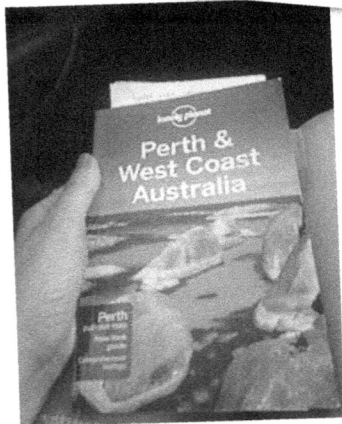

Perth &
West Coast
Australia

Adventures in
Western Australia

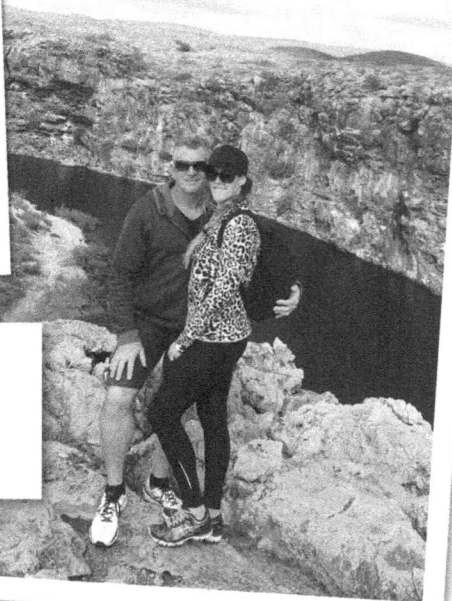

FINDING THE RIGHT FORMULA

Once the haze of depression clears, the natural next step is to experiment with alternative paths and identities that can exist outside of the previous expectations. For Jed and me, picking up our whole lives was a drastic experimentation but very much necessary and a risk that paid off! Being able to leave the environment that was plagued in grief and into one that was so full of new experiences and adventures was essential to our healing process, and it allowed us to build lives outside of the expectations we had held onto for so long.

This stage of your life is all about trial and error. Find out what brings you genuine joy and fulfillment, gather evidence, and build new hopes for the future (although these don't have to be permanent!). This is the testing era, where you're exploring new pathways while gradually building your confidence. The freedom of all the different possibilities should feel empowering and relieving.

While you're in this testing phase, it's okay if you feel:

- Uncertain or unsettled, like you're not sure which direction to take

- Guilty for feeling happy

- Excited and overwhelmed by all the new possibilities

- Disconnected from your old self

- Afraid of making a 'wrong' move

When you're embedded in the experiment stage, it can be confusing to sort out which of these new experiences truly fulfills you. It can be helpful to keep a journal where you record your thoughts after each experience and track what energises or drains you. Ask yourself questions like: In which situations did I feel most like myself and why? What am I curious to try, even if I'm not sure I'll be good at it? What fears or assumptions might be holding me back from exploring something new?

The more pathways you experiment with, the more you cross off the list until you find the one that is right for you.

CHAPTER 7

HELLO, THIS IS ANGER SPEAKING

When the dream
is murdered,
rage writes
the eulogy.

In September 2013, my biological clock was ticking and I couldn't help but feel like time was moving fast and my window was closing. The thought of being 32 was scary, especially as a female. Our age plays a significant role in our fertility, as our eggs age with us. So yes, my eggs were also 32 years old now. For the past 18 months, Jed and I had been living our dream life on the beautiful beaches of Western Australia. We'd explored places like Margaret River, Augusta, Cape Naturaliste, Pinnacles, Shark Bay, and Monkey Mia, and we feel incredibly blessed to have had this opportunity. For the first time in a long while, I finally felt like myself again. Working every other week had been like winning the lottery! With this newfound sense of vitality, we realised that if we didn't take action now, we might never do it.

Driven by my innate desire for change, we opened the door again and decided to embark on another cycle of IVF – our 7th cycle of fertility treatments. This was not a decision we made lightly, as anyone who has undergone IVF can attest to the emotional and physical toll it can exact, and given our past experience, we were extremely aware of how hard and long the road could be. However, our time in WA had healed us. We felt a sense of calm and I was healthier, happier, and I'd started to pull those walls down and remove the expectations of our Sydney life. I felt free. We'd become different people, but at the same time, we'd also remembered who we were as a couple before the fertility chaos began. At this point we thought that moving to WA was the missing piece and it was now our chance to become parents. I honestly believed that the tide had turned, and I was in such a better place emotionally to become a mum.

After thorough research, we selected a reputable clinic in Perth and set off on this journey with cautious hope. The initial months were a whirlwind of appointments, treatments, and interminable waiting. We relied on each other for support, finding solace in the knowledge that we were in this together, regardless of the outcome. The process was arduous, but it also brought us closer, fortifying our bond in unforeseen ways. In between treatments, we took the opportunity to explore our new home. Perth offered an abundance of treasures: pristine beaches, bustling markets, and a warm and welcoming community. We stumbled upon hidden gems in the city, from charming coffee shops to picturesque hiking trails, each outing becoming a cherished remembrance.

After being referred to a renowned clinic, we met with a doctor who had been in the field since before I was even born. He was direct and no-nonsense, and after reviewing our history, he couldn't find any obvious issues. So, we decided to give IVF another go. However, with both of us working as FIFO (fly-in fly-out) workers, scheduling appointments and injections became quite challenging. But we were determined to make it work. Looking back, I feel foolish for not being open and honest with my employer about my need for time off. I believe one of my managers may have known, but I was so secretive about my whereabouts when I needed to change flights and my work rotation to accommodate tests and scans. As I get older, I regret not prioritising my own needs and consistently putting myself last.

✳ ✳ ✳

I got the call just after I had finished with another transvaginal scan. I am no stranger to these tests; they had become a routine part of my life at this point. The initial discomfort and embarrassment had given way to a numbness I never thought was possible. Yet, despite the frequency of these scans, I still couldn't help but feel a glimmer of hope every time I went in for one. Each scan was another step in the journey towards starting a family with Jed. As I walked to the car, my phone rang but I missed the call.

My heart skipped a beat when I saw it was from the clinic. I quickly called back, my mind racing with a million different thoughts. When the receptionist answered and put me through to the GP at the clinic, I could hear the hesitation in her voice. My stomach dropped as she started to tell me about the initial test results. This testing process was always standard when you start with a new clinic, but it brought back old memories and wounds. Memories flooded back and anxiety set in while we waited for those results, hoping and praying that nothing untoward was uncovered. My mind immediately jumped to worst-case scenarios, but then she said the words that filled me with immense relief: Jed had the all-clear. My eyes filled with tears and a weight lifted off my shoulders as I continued walking through the car park, scanning for my car.

I felt fine, until the GP hesitated again. My heart dropped once more as I wondered what the problem could be. She finally told me that the fibroid I had been diagnosed with was nothing to worry about. I let out a small laugh, feeling foolish for getting worked up over something so insignificant. In the grand scheme of things, the fibroid was a minor hurdle in our journey towards starting a family. With Jed's good health and this reassurance from the GP, I knew that we could overcome anything together.

Another moment passed and she paused. *Wait there's more?* I was still wandering aimlessly trying to find the car when the GP said with a voice full of concern and pity, "Kelly, our initial tests confirm..." She hesitated and I felt my heart racing and my hands shake as I waited for her to continue. *What could it possibly be now?* "Kelly, you have a chromosome disorder," she finally said, her words hanging heavily in the air. I stood there while she explained what this meant, utterly frozen in time as the weight of her words sunk in.

My mind was racing, trying to process what this could mean for my future. Tears started to stream down my face, and I somehow managed to get to the car and collapse inside. I felt so alone and lost, with only my thoughts and fears to keep me company. She told me I have a Robertsonian trans-location that affected my 13th and 14th chromosomes (yes, 13!). Humans generally have 46 chromosomes altogether, but this condition meant that my 13th and 14th chromo-somes had fused and caused an error in my DNA chain. Long story short, the prognosis for pregnancy is not positive and people with Robertsonian translocation have difficulty getting pregnant and are at a higher risk of miscarriages.

My world was spinning, and I was trying to grasp what was going on, struggling to find a tissue to wipe away my tears. *Oh god… how will I tell Jed?* I sobbed my heart out, with people passing by my car, looking in and walking away from this crazy lady hysterically crying. I just wished Jed was here, but he was away at work and wouldn't be back for another week. I missed him so much, like I'd never missed him before. Through my blurry, sobbing eyes, I managed to call him and break the yet again devastating news. He was so calm, brave, and positive, just like he always was. Once again, he was my rock, my anchor in this storm of emotions.

I left the car park and drove home, but I don't remember getting there that day. I don't remember the drive or much else that followed in the weeks after. I felt like I was living in a nightmare, one that I could never seem to wake up from. I'd become accustomed to pushing my feelings aside just to make it through another day, but with this new diagnosis, I didn't know if I'd be able to keep going.

✳ ✳ ✳

We were in a state of shock and disbelief when we found out I had a chromosomal abnormality. The news hit us like a tonne of bricks, and we were suddenly thrust into a situation we had never anticipated. Amid our grief and confusion, we couldn't think straight, and it was difficult to make any decisions. All we could do was try to understand what this diagnosis meant and how it would impact our lives. We were overwhelmed and didn't know where to turn for help. Looking back, I often wonder why we didn't take more action against the original clinics that didn't perform the necessary tests. If we had, maybe we could have prevented other couples from going through the same heartache. But it was hard to think clearly and we were consumed with anger towards the system.

CHAPTER 7

This was a whole different level of emotion. The rage I felt was new to me. I hadn't felt this kind of despair, resentment, anger all rolled into one before. Even after six previous rounds of fertility treatments and multiple miscarriages, so many questions were still unravelling in my mind, and I didn't know how to process this. My expectations again severed from my reality, and we were left to deal with the consequences of a process we thought we fully understood but now evidently just felt was driven by money. We focused all our energy on understanding the severity of the condition and trying to come to terms with it. However, I can't help but feel regret for not standing up and asking the tough questions that could have made a difference for others in the future. I wish I had the strength and clarity to fight back, but at the time, it just seemed like we were driving through thick fog with no headlights and no guide.

I can understand what you may be thinking: How could it take three clinics, countless doctors, and 8 years of trying to finally discover my genetic chromosome disorder? I never in my wildest dreams thought this is where we'd be after years of trying to conceive. We trusted and believed our doctors, the nurses, and every clinic we'd been to see. We trusted every blood test, every scan and every person who told us we had hope. But even with all that trust, we were still left with empty arms and broken hearts. We put our faith in the very doctor who confidently said, "I don't see why you won't be pregnant within the year." We clung to those words, holding onto the hope that our dreams of parenthood would finally come true. My expectations were built around every one of those conversations with specialists. But our expectations and trust were shattered in one fell swoop. A diagnosis of a chromosome disorder so late in our journey left us reeling. We were left questioning everything – every process, every person, every hope. We became cynical and sceptical, doubting even the very air we breathed. Our journey had taken a toll on us, changing us as individuals and as a couple. To this day, I struggle to fully comprehend how that period truly changed me. It was a transformation, a shedding of the naive and trusting person I once was. I became more guarded, more cautious, more hesitant to put my trust in anyone or anything. The pain of our journey still lingers, a constant reminder of the fragility of trust and the expectations we put on ourselves.

It's hard to believe that clinics can have such different processes. Chromosome testing wasn't really something they discussed as a vital test in your early days with these clinics, and only the most common chromosome disorders are tested for like the Down syndrome gene. You can imagine the rage when you're now at your third clinic that actually has a testing regime that uncovers this abnormality, yet if the first two had the same, we could've had answers 8 years prior.

The power and the potential change these clinics could have on people's lives if information was shared and standardised is immense.

Looking back, I wish we had known to do more research and question everything. We were so eager to start our journey to parenthood that we didn't even think to ask why certain tests were being done or why we were following a specific process or even do all clinics offer the same testing? It's frustrating to think that we could have saved ourselves years of heartache if we had just taken a simple blood test to check for any chromosome-related issues. It's scary to think that we were blindly trusting these clinics to guide us in the right direction. I can't help but wonder if our outcome would have been different if we had taken a more proactive approach and questioned the process from the beginning. In the end, I learned that no matter what clinic or hospital you go to, you have to be your own advocate. You have to ask why and do your own research. Trust your instincts and don't be afraid to speak up. It's your body and your journey, and you deserve to have all the answers and information to make the best decisions for yourself and your future family. This monumental mistake taught me the importance of being proactive and taking control of my own fertility journey. I hope that by sharing my story, I can bring awareness to the need for more detailed chromosome testing and save other couples from experiencing the same pain and regret that we did.

As I've continually grown, I've learned to believe the old saying that "everything happens for a reason." As awful as this period was, it gave us an understanding of what had been happening but also shaped who I am today. I know I'm a stronger person because of this one thing, I know I'm more confident to step up when I need to, and I know I will never again not speak up for what is right.

∗ ∗ ∗

Despite the challenges of working away and navigating appointments, Jed and I discussed with the doctors the process to move forward. What would continuing with IVF now look like for us? Is it even viable? Once a chromosome disorder is discovered, there are various options to consider, so Jed and I decided to give it one more shot. In 2013/2014, we were introduced to a new process we had never heard of before – genetic testing on the embryo. We had to meet with counsellors and specialists to fully understand the process and make informed decisions for our future. This involved fertilising our eggs and sending them to a laboratory for testing. However, this process was not easy, and we had to go through the exhausting IVF process with the added stress of ruling out any eggs with the disorder. To even reach this stage, we had to apply to the government to allow us to choose our own embryo, as we ultimately had to choose which ones to fertilise and discard any that may contain the gene.

We underwent the gruelling process of retrieving and fertilising the precious eggs, enduring a rollercoaster of emotions and anxious waiting. Our hearts were filled with hope and anticipation as we prepared to implant them back into my womb, praying for the miracle of pregnancy. But alas, our dreams were shattered on the third day when we received the devastating news that my remaining eggs were not viable. After previous experiences with hyperstimulation, we made the devastating decision to abort the cycle. It was a crushing blow, a monumental moment that marked the end of our journey. The weight of our disappointment and loss was unbearable, and we knew we could not handle any further challenges.

With heavy hearts, we sought the guidance of our doctor at the clinic who was a renowned expert in the field. He was a mysterious and enigmatic figure, and his piercing gaze seemed to see right through us. His deep, gravelly voice was intimidating, but we hung onto his every word, hoping for some sort of explanation or solution. But as he spoke, it became clear that our fate was sealed. The complexity of our situation and the depth of our despair was palpable in the air. Our senses were overwhelmed – the smell of disinfectant and fear, the sound of machines and whispers, the sight of sterile white walls and tear-streaked cheeks. It was a moment that would forever be etched in our memories, a pivotal moment that changed the course of our lives.

The only statement I remember from that meeting was, "Are you prepared to spend the rest of your lives without children?" The words echoed in my mind, each syllable piercing my heart like a knife. They brought back the memory of the last 8 years, a constant battle of hope and disappointment, of trying and failing. And in that moment, all that pain and loss was summed up in that one line. Sitting there, lifeless and defeated, I tried to put on a brave face. But inside, I was crumbling. My heart ached with a pain I had never felt before. I sobbed in the car with Jed. He held me, his strong arms providing some solace, but he couldn't take away the emptiness I felt. This was it. The end of the road. After everything we had been through, all the medical procedures and emotional turmoil, my body had done all it could. I had done all I could. And yet, it still wasn't enough. I couldn't help but wonder, *what were we going to do now?* The thought of spending the rest of our lives without children was unbearable. It was a loss that cut deep, leaving a void in my heart that I didn't know how to fill. As we continued to put on our brave faces and pick ourselves up as we always did, I couldn't shake the feeling of being lost. It was the most lost I had ever felt. I had lost all hope. And without hope, I had nothing. Jed could see it too. He could see that I was broken, and he felt helpless.

One night, while we were on a break from the mine site, he took me down to the sunset at Scarborough beach. He knew how much I loved sunsets, how they were like my medicine. There was something about watching the sun set over the water in Western Australia that brought me peace. Maybe it was because it was the only place where I could feel truly free. We sat there, watching the sun slowly dip below the horizon, painting the sky with hues of pink and orange. Jed looked at me with concern in his eyes and said, "I'm worried you're broken, and for the life of me, I don't know how to fix you." In that moment, I knew he was right. I was broken. And I didn't know how to put myself back together.

"In all this time, I've never seen you this way." His words echoed in my mind, a constant reminder of the shattered pieces of my soul. I never thought I would be in this position, childless and lost. I had always believed that we would have children, that we would find our way to parenthood. But now, staring at the dead end before us, I was completely shattered. Jed's eyes met mine, and I could see the pain reflected in them. He felt broken, just like me. I hated that he had to be the one to fix me, as if it were his responsibility. But at that moment, I couldn't deny my brokenness. I was shattered, and I didn't know how to put myself back together.

I hadn't yet embraced or accepted the cards we'd been dealt. It felt like there was still so much to understand and accept, but I knew at this point something needed to change. It was such a pivotal point in my life, and I know you'll also experience moments like this. It's an unconscious moment where choices need to be made for your survival, and this could honestly change the trajectory of your life. I urge you to take the leap into the unknown and challenge yourself with something you never thought might be possible. I bet you'll surprise yourself.

JED'S PERSPECTIVE

We are now firmly entrenched in the WA lifestyle, and we wouldn't change a thing. For us, Perth is the happy medium between Kelly being the city girl and myself preferring the country lifestyle. Perth, we have found, offers both. We both found a part ourselves over here that was missing back east and more importantly, we reconnected.

But after the diagnosis and final IVF attempt, there were some very dark times that even now I find hard to express properly. Being an extremely private person, and I'll admit, dealing with these strong emotions is not my forte, I felt the best way to deal with the mounting issues was to concentrate solely on the well-being of Kelly. I did what I could to ease any anxiety or frustrations that Kelly went through; however, there was a point in all this where I said to Kelly out of such helplessness and utter desperation, "You're broken and I don't know how to fix you?" We didn't know at the time how profound that statement would be. It jolted Kelly into a mindset that she needed to accept the reality of it all and start making the rest of her life into the best version she could or drown in self-pity that would eventually consume her and possibly, us.

It happened overnight. A change in Kelly that was emphasised by determination and resolve, which were traits that had attracted me to her originally and were starting to resurface. I liken Kelly, with total respect, to a dog with a bone. Once she has made up her mind, there aren't a lot of things that will stop her. She embarked on a new career journey while holding down a superintendent job with a mining company. I couldn't be prouder as she took that discipline by storm and is now considered one of the leading businesses in that field, not only in WA but Australia. What has made me even prouder is how Kelly has accepted the cards she was dealt with and moved past it all to be the woman she is today. What has helped me to accept our fertility fate too was watching Kelly break down every other barrier put before her. I won't lie, I still have the odd dark moment and contemplate the what ifs, but her strength has helped me heal as well.

LISTENING TO WHAT ANGER HAS TO SAY

In this period of my life, it was as if we had gone through all the stages all over again. Bargaining, shock, denial, depression and then finally anger. Anger was underneath it all though. At the unfairness of it, for starters. *Why me?* Out of all the things that could be slightly abnormal with my body, why did it have to be something so small that had such massive consequences? There was also a lot of anger at all the clinics we had been at previously. Their lack of care and due diligence caused us years of continual heartbreak, and that also didn't feel fair.

The anger stage often arrives with a heat that surprises us – not just because of its intensity, but because of how long it's been building beneath the surface. It can appear multiple times throughout this journey, as most of them will. But when it truly hits, it's the part of grief where the loss feels personal, targeted, unjust. Suddenly, the narrative shifts from heartbreak to protest: *Why me? Why this? Why now?* Anger in this stage can be wildly misdirected or perfectly focused. It might be aimed at society as a whole, certain individuals, groups of your family and friends, or the systems that failed you. And sometimes, most brutally, the anger turns inward – at your body, your decisions, your hopefulness, your perceived inadequacies.

**If you're in the depths of anger,
it's okay if you feel:**

- That your anger is bigger than you know how to handle

- Torn between wanting to scream and wanting to cry

- Betrayed by your body, your intuition, your past choices, or even your hope

- Like you need someone to blame, even if there's no clear culprit

For many, this is the moment where grief morphs into something sharper, more active. It's a refusal to accept what happened as just 'one of those things'. It's the brain and body fighting to reclaim some sense of power, even if the only power available is shouting at the universe. Anger often means you're finally being honest with yourself about the depth of your loss.

CHAPTER 8

ACCEPTING THE UNIVERSE'S EDITS

Even the greatest written masterpieces
have had major edits.

"It's hard to describe the feeling that
comes with starting your own business.

It really is so much work in the
beginning that you lose yourself in
it. You lose your sense of time, you
can't believe how quickly the days go
because there really is no time to focus
on anything else.

But then you open the doors and it's
like you have given birth to this new
thing that didn't exist before. But then
when it starts to flourish, well that's the
icing on the cake.

To get to see it, live it and breathe and
to know that this thing you created
out of thin air can put a smile on other
people's faces is a blessing."

Joanna Gaines, *The Magnolia Story*

The words, "I know you're broken, and I don't know how to fix you" will be forever etched in my mind. Jed knew I was at rock bottom. I was broken but what I didn't realise was that he thought it was his job to fix me. I'd always been a strong independent person, and I was heartbroken to think he had that weight on his shoulders, trying to pick himself up but also trying to pick me up along the way too. It's crazy how as couples we often forget how each of us affects our other halves and the responsibility we put on ourselves.

Weeks passed and turned into months, but the ache in my heart remained. I tried everything to distract myself – kinesiology, exercise, reading – but nothing could ease the pain of this new reality. I needed time to help me move forward. As I struggled to find a sense of purpose and self-worth, I realised that our society puts too much emphasis on the 'ticking the box' lifestyle. Get a good job, get married, have a nice house, a white picket fence, and kids. It's like these things are what define us as adults.

I couldn't help but feel frustrated when strangers would ask me about children within the first few questions. Have you ever noticed as a woman when you meet new people, through business or personal reasons, it could even be a networking event or a friend's party that the conversation will always quickly deviate to your 'status'. Questions are quickly asked around: "Are you married?" and "Do you have children?" It raises the perception that my worth as a woman is dictated by these two questions, and when I respond no to children, it's as if that was my choice and I would be judged for that. In my early days and during the depths of our fertility struggles, I would dread meeting new people as I knew this would be an area of discussion or I'd end up in a circle of women talking about their children and feel like I couldn't contribute value to the conversation because I hadn't experienced being a mother.

But life had thrown me a curveball, and I had to figure out what road to take. Would I sit in the corner, directionless and lost, and continue with my job in mining? Or would I find a new path, one that would give me purpose and direction?

I needed a challenge, something to keep my mind busy and to make me feel like I was achieving something. After researching different courses, one kept calling out to me: interior design. Around the same time, Jed and I had decided to officially settle in WA by buying a block to build our dream home on. I had no idea what the future held, but I knew that I needed to take a chance and pursue this new passion and do something for me.

Studying design was an outlet for me in between my mining rotations. I'd found something creative that I enjoyed and coupled with starting to plan our new home build, I'd found something that was mine – this was for me. I'd finally felt like I was creating something that was amazing and hey, I was good at it! I'd been failing and falling for such a long time now and this love for design was new and it inspired something different in me, something that I hadn't felt in a long time. For the first time in a long time, I put zero expectations on myself to achieve anything. I was simply enjoying the moment, and I'd honestly forgotten what that had felt like.

I started my business as a side hustle first, with a dream of being creative and to give my mind a focus out of all the despair. I didn't start with grand plans, huge goals, or a 10-year agenda. I just started. And for anyone thinking you need all the systems and processes to get off the ground like a person who has been doing it for 20 years, I can tell you that you don't. Just start. It's as simple as that. Get out of your own way and just start.

When I'd completed my studies and we'd moved into our dream home, I was working in a high level role in mining. At this point, I hadn't even registered a business name, thought about a website or even where'd I'd begin. But strangely I wasn't even worried. I think because I'd honestly had zero expectations of what I was doing, I hadn't built myself up to potentially fail either. I remember thinking this will be years down the road anyway if I potentially start something, so I'd just do a couple of things on the side over the years and enjoy the ride.

I started with the basics and worked with my best friend on her new apartment transformation. I put her visions into a mood board, we shopped like she was my client, and I was in my element. It was so fun, and I was filled with enthusiasm to create her dream. What I loved the most was that I was helping her. I'd forgotten so much about myself at this point. I'd forgotten what I was good at and how so many of my career choices had actually gotten me to this point without even realising it. But seeing how I'd helped change her life gave me a feeling of hope. The shattered pieces were starting to repair in the most unexpected way.

I laugh now looking back at the start of what was going to be the next big chapter of my life. There was no grand epiphany that sparked my vision. It was a simple desire to indulge in my passion, to create something for myself. But as I reflect on my journey and now mentor students, I realise that my 'why' was solely focused on me. It was my personal need for a creative outlet, a goal to strive for, and a sense of purpose that drove me forward. But my 'why' was also about helping others. I was creating a space to lead and guide others, whether it was their home or business.

Now, I don't recommend starting a business without thorough research. I had not investigated my competitors, found a gap in the market, or discovered a niche. I hadn't even considered how I would balance this venture with my demanding job in the mining industry. But I knew deep down that this was meant for me. Whether it was just a hobby or a full-fledged business, I was determined to make it happen.

When you start a business, you need a name. I knew I wanted it to be different, no surprises there, but I didn't want it to be named after me since the number of times I've heard my surname mispronounced is more than the times it has been pronounced right. I wanted something with meaning, but at the time I didn't even realise the impact of having a brand and not just a name too.

After Jed and I came up with all different types of options, we couldn't go past the number 13. It had always held a significant role in my life – buying a house on the 13th, proposing on the 13th, getting married on the 13th, my disorder on the 13th chromosome, even being seated at table 13 in restaurants. And now, my husband and I both have 13 tattoos. For better or for worse, 13 has always been by my side in some way.

This number has followed us, and it had meaning. When it came to interior design, I also realised that there were 12 key elements and principles of design in my course, so if I combined the 12 elements of design with my client, that equalled 13. And so, 13 Interiors was born, and it has continued to evolve ever since.

On February 19, 2017, I sat on our new balcony with a cup of tea looking over the ocean and registered my business name, then quickly realised I'd better check I can get the domain and Instagram page too. Told you I didn't really have a plan... thankfully over 38k social media followers later, I can assure you I am the key holder of the 13 Interiors name and brand.

✳ ✳ ✳

As I reflect on my childhood, I realise that I was destined to be a creative soul. It was always there, lurking beneath the surface and waiting to be unleashed. I had a love for design and styling, and family and friends always said I had a natural flair for it, even from my childhood days of my red, blue and yellow tulip themed bedroom. But it wasn't until I grew older that I truly understood the depth of my creativity.

My family tree was filled with creative genes, and I was no exception. My mother, a talented seamstress, was my first inspiration. She created stunning wedding gowns and brides-maid dresses, pouring her heart and soul into every stitch. I remember watching her work in awe, and I was lucky enough to have her create my own wedding dress years later.

But beyond her incredible talent, she also built her own successful business from scratch. She did it all while raising my brother and me, always making sure she was there for us when we needed her. I don't think she fully grasps the magnitude of what she accomplished, but as someone who runs my own business now, I understand the immense dedication and hard work it takes. I also had another creative influence – my aunt. She was a performer with a beautiful voice, and her photography skills were unmatched. Looking back, I had no idea how much these two influential figures shaped my creative path.

But creativity alone doesn't give you the ability to sustain and manage a business long term. I knew I also got that drive from my dad. Dad has a keen business eye and was an extremely hard worker. Once he gets an idea, he sees it through to the very end. I know my relentless drive to succeed comes from him, as his work and dedication for the company he worked decades for never went unnoticed. Dad and mum provided a life for my brother and I that they could only dream of growing up and one that I'm very grateful for and probably don't tell them enough. So, thank you Mum and Dad for providing a world for us that would have tested you many times over.

One of my biggest inspirations is Joanna Gaines, the renowned house flipping guru and author. Her words from her book *The Magnolia Story* resonate with me deeply and serve as a constant reminder that I am on the right path.

I wonder if we know ourselves a lot better than we think we do when we are children. We get into our teen years and college years, and so many of us let others redefine who we are or we get lost along the way and have no idea what we want to really do with our lives. But once we figure it out, it often seems easy to look back at our childhood and find clues that say, "Hey, maybe you were headed in that direction all along."

I often ponder over this quote, reflecting on the subtle hints my childhood gave about my future path. Whether it was spending hours doodling in my notebooks, rearranging my bedroom furniture to create the perfect space, or helping my mum select fabrics and patterns for her latest creations, the signs were there all along. These small acts of creativity were more than just hobbies; they were the building blocks of my future career.

✳ ✳ ✳

Starting 13 Interiors was a huge milestone. I'd come through so much at this point. We'd uprooted our life to WA, worked in the remote regions of the desolate Pilbara in the blazing heat, went through a horrific diagnosis and fate on our journey to start a family, and built a home. All in the space of 5 years. I never in a million years thought this is where I'd be. I also never thought I'd start to see a light. The light of hope that there was something else for me that was mine and something that I'd created. 13 Interiors was all for me and my creative way of helping others. It truly has always been about creating a dream home for people and to change the way they live their lives, and to this moment I can truly say I'm proud of each and every client I've worked with and what has been created for them.

When the business started to take off and I had some referrals coming in from the builder who built our home, I started to gain more exposure to the design world and the networks within, but also the networks of the small business scene in Perth. This truly opened my eyes to the depth that was needed to potentially grow this business and brand.

At this time, I'd been in a lot of roles, which honestly, I could write another book about this alone! I'd started out my working journey after high school teaching children to swim and my big break came when I was hired to set up a swim school from scratch at 19 years old. Me, at 19, setting up a business structure and employing staff. It feels crazy saying this, but it's honestly the truth. My career progressed to a national role at this company before I moved into local government running programs with up to 50 staff and over

4000 participants per week in my programs. Those two roles spanned over 13 years and I'm forever grateful for the learnings and opportunities that came from that.

Mining was a huge curveball. I remember my first day on site in early 2012, navigating the huge camp while dragging my trolley bag through the rocks and gravel to find my 'donga'. I'd never even been camping, so this was an eye opener. I remember tears rolling down my face periodically in those first few weeks thinking, *what have I done leaving the safety of Sydney and a consistent job*? But I knew we'd come here for more than just work. It was a total life reset.

I'm proud of what I learnt in this mining career, the systems and processes I created, and the culture I instilled in the teams that worked for me. That place made me stronger, and in some ways, maybe it prepared me for the chromosome diagnosis. I learnt what it was like to work hard in a whole different sense. For people that think working 12–14-hour days in a remote site and living away from home is easy because of the money, it's not. It comes with a whole set of challenges. But I know I wouldn't change a thing. I met the most inspiring people on this path.

I now know that all these roles led me to be the person I am, and each and every part of these roles has made me a better leader, mentor, communicator and given me the confidence to build 13 Interiors. I often hear people say to me that

I came out of nowhere when I started 13, but it was the years of hustle that taught me the skills of how to build this brand along with some very inspiring mentors in the early days.

It's always an interesting conversation when people ask about my previous jobs and how I'm suddenly an interior designer. I often sense their assumption is that I get bored easily or maybe I couldn't hold down a job? The bored part probably has some truth to it! I do believe that I crave diversity and change now. Because I've experienced so much change and my expectations are constantly reset, I see the diversity in my previous roles as a huge positive. Every one of my roles came with a different set of managers who each taught me something new. In particular, my first management role with Fitness First taught me so much about autonomy and independence. I was basically setting up a swim school from scratch with no real guidance on what I was supposed to do. Moving into my local government role progressed me to a whole new level of responsibility. Larger teams, workplace culture issues, clientele expectations. New pressure meant adapting to new ways of doing things. Every one of these roles taught me something new and you will never hear me say I regret any of the paths that I went down or how I left these roles either. As they say, never burn your bridges and I believe that to its truest form.

If you're starting on your business journey or thinking

about a career change, it is never too late to start anything. I am living proof that by having a why and just starting can mean the most amazing things can often unfold. Never underestimate the power of your previous careers or life moments in shaping the way you do things moving forward. All these moments led me to where I am now. Limiting yourself and your beliefs is the only thing stopping you.

✳ ✳ ✳

Initially, I juggled running my business side by side with my mining career. I spent time researching, networking, and connecting with other knowledgeable individuals in the small business world. But as I delved deeper, I quickly realised I needed to up my game and project a professional image if I wanted to compete with the big guns in the Perth design scene. And without tooting my own horn, I knew I had the talent and drive to do it. After years of fixing and starting other people's businesses, it was finally time to create something of my own.

By the end of 2017, our dream home was complete – a stunning masterpiece perched on a cliff overlooking the sparkling waters below. The glass windows stretched high into the sky, offering breathtaking views from every angle. It was like living in a luxurious glass castle, and every day I woke up feeling grateful and in awe. Betty, my dear friend, had been right all along. She had encouraged me to take the leap, and now I couldn't thank her enough. The build process was a labour of love. I poured my heart and soul into every detail, using all the knowledge and skills I had gained from my courses. Our home reflected all the things I loved in design, with modern contemporary materials and finishes and some dark and moody moments in the aesthetic. My style was being born, and I didn't even realise it yet.

After our home was finished, I knew I needed more projects that sparked this same energy in me, so I set the wheels in motion to make my dream business a reality. I staged a full photo shoot in my new home, collaborating with five businesses in Perth to showcase their products and my styling. It was a whirlwind of creative energy and hard work, resulting in 100 professionally photographed styled images that would soon be circulating the social media scene. With my portfolio finally kickstarted, I launched a new website featuring my work and gained instant exposure on social media.

Within just eight months, my following on Instagram alone had grown to over 5000 – a feat that any Instagrammer knows is incredibly challenging. The skills I'd learnt previously in business had become transferable without even realising it. My marketing skills from Fitness First and local government days were helping me build a brand. I knew how important these elements were to a business. My communication skills were being tested to their highest degree and again I had realised that the experiences in mining and working in such a diverse culture with a huge range of demographics had also become transferable to this newfound design career. I was immensely proud of what I had accomplished, and the evidence was clear that people were noticing it as enquiries started to flood in. A different style was being set in Perth, and I had created it. But I wasn't finished testing myself yet. I decided to teach myself photography, both to save on costs and to have the ability to photograph my work as soon as it was finished. It was multi-tasking at its finest to push the landscape of my business even further. In my first full year as a small business owner, I made a six-figure salary and worked with 45 clients.

My work was featured by prestigious brands such as Snooze Australia, *News.com.au*, *Domain.com.au*, and *Minty Magazine*, and I even got the opportunity to be interviewed on 6PR radio. On top of all that, I managed to balance this success with a full-time job as a regional mining superinten-dent. But as proud as I was of my achievements, I couldn't deny the toll it was taking on me. Work was becoming my entire life, and the juggling act was starting to wear me down. In a sense, I was still masking pain and coming to grips with the cards that we had been dealt, but I was on the path to healing.

Building our home in
Western Australia

On site

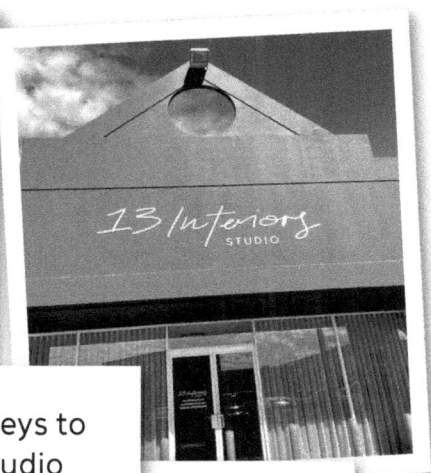

Getting the keys to
the Perth studio

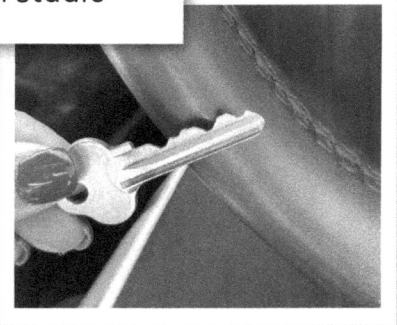

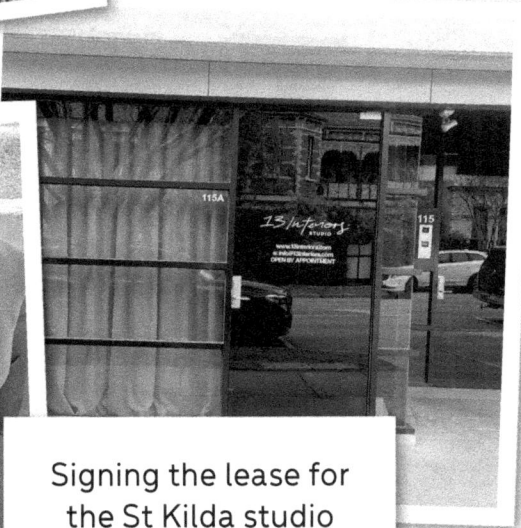

Signing the lease for
the St Kilda studio

As 2018 rolled in like a cyclone, I was caught up in the chaos. Everything fell into place, and I finally felt like I was on the right path, despite my fears of leaving the security of my mining job. The uncertainty was overwhelming, but I believed we could overcome it, just like we had with past challenges. Jed, always supportive, stood by me through it all.

But then, the brakes screeched to a halt when my sister-in-law called with devastating news. My brother, just 34 years old, had been diagnosed with cancer. It was a harrowing journey for all of us. The treatment process and recovery period were tough on him, his wife, our parents, me, and Jed. It was a challenging and uncertain time, with the fear of losing him weighing heavily on our minds.

It was also a wake-up call that forced me to re-evaluate my priorities and put my life and family first. I couldn't ignore the fact that my work had consumed me, and it was time to find a better balance. After my brother recovered from surgery and treatment, he said something that was the final push: "Why are you doing two jobs? I think what you are doing is a 'thing.'" It took my younger brother to put things into perspective in the simplest way. I was running myself ragged and I honestly didn't need my mining job anymore.

Jed was also in agreement that I was working myself to the bone and something needed to change. It's amazing that deep down inside you already know it though. You know that you can't continue to try and be everything to everyone. It was at this point I realised I'd completely changed my trajectory. All the years of expectations for the life I thought I was going to live had changed. I had built something entirely different, and it was my own version of the white-picket-fence story. I was removing the limitations that I'd set for myself and come out the other side of a horrendous chapter that largely involved me trying to live a life that society expected of me. I'd challenged everything thrown at me and embraced a completely different path. I now needed to go all in and prove that anything is possible. What would be the point if I didn't?

In the months before this, I had already thought about why I started this business and the journey that got me here so far. Life had dealt us some truly crappy cards, but I persevered and created something amazing. A business born from passion and purpose, changing lives through design and styling. And the characters in this story? Well, they're just as complex and intriguing as the rollercoaster of life itself. I found my why and that gave everything meaning. It provided me with so much clarity about what I was supposed to be doing. I knew in my soul this was where I was supposed to be. I found my purpose and drive to keep pushing forward, no matter how tough the road may be. And in the end, it was the simplest words from my brother that put everything into perspective.

By far one of the most common questions I'm asked is, "When did you know it was time to take the leap?" It's usually one of the biggest hurdles anyone embarking on their own business journey will face. The leap from one stable income stream into the small business world where there is no backing and you are your own boss. The truth is no one will ever be able to do this for you. They won't be able to give you this answer and there is no amount of wishing and praying to guide you into the next chapter and provide that security and ultimately answer that question for you. This quote by Estee Lauder sums it up perfectly: "I didn't get there by wishing for it or hoping for it, but by working for it." You'll know when the moment is right, and all the signs are there. You'll embrace the change, and you'll look back and wonder why you didn't do it sooner.

Life was never meant to be easy, and not everyone is destined to have a traditional life. Despite having a chromosome disorder that is a permanent part of my life, I have come to accept and embrace it. It's crucial for society to understand that everyone's journey is unique, and it's unfair to judge others based on external appearances and perceptions. Not having children does not define our worth or happiness; it is perfectly acceptable to be ourselves – a regular couple not bound by societal expectations. This is my story, and it's one that evokes a multitude of emotions – fear, love, hope, and resilience. And I wouldn't have it any other way.

REACHING ACCEPTANCE

Acceptance isn't about being 'over it', it's about learning how to live with it. It's the steady realisation that while the life you imagined didn't happen, the life you're living now holds value, meaning, and perhaps even joy. In this stage, there's a sense of emotional integration: the loss doesn't vanish, but it becomes part of your story rather than the whole story. You stop fighting what isn't and begin building what is.

For me, acceptance looked like not only closing and locking the door on motherhood, but also walking away from it completely through another door. I poured myself into my interior design business, and in doing so, I found another version of my future that I had never considered before. This didn't erase the loss, but it expanded my understanding of fulfillment and how different versions of my timeline could exist.

This stage is also about telling your story differently – not as a failure or detour, but as a path that was painful, yes, but also powerful. You rewrite what success looks like on your own terms and something shifts. You no longer feel out of place in a world that celebrates traditional milestones. You learn to carry your truth confidently, even if it doesn't match the blueprint. Acceptance is standing tall in your chosen life and saying, *this is still mine.*

When you reach acceptance, it's okay if you feel:

- Guilty for moving on and being happy

- Grateful for your past experiences, even if they were hurtful

- Occasionally angry or sad about the path behind you

- Uncertain or doubtful at times about your future

This chapter is about my advice to you. The unexpected advice you didn't know you needed. Review my reflections below and think about your own answers. You don't need to share this with anyone. It's about being true to yourself without being tainted by anyone else's beliefs of what your path should look like. Remember that your white picket fence doesn't need to be the same as your neighbours. It's your journey.

**When I strip back what people think
I should do, what is my truth?**

At this moment in time, I felt like I needed to be
in a typical career that was 9–5. I was dealing
with the emotions of not being a mother and
what that road would look like. I thought
following my passion may compromise our
quality of life and leave my husband pressured
to be the income earner. I was scared to leave
the security of the full-time role.

What obstacles do I see in my way?

Job security and what will people
think of me if I fail.

**What are 2–3 things I want to
change and embrace?**

My perception of failure and job security.

The reality of this exercise is to show you that in the big picture, perception is what you make it. Wouldn't you be prouder knowing you tried and possibly failed than if you didn't try at all?

CHAPTER 9

THRIVING IN A LIFE YOU'VE DESIGNED

Moving forward is
reliant on reconciling
who we thought
we were with who
we actually are.

f I'd limited my beliefs to what I thought I was capable of achieving and didn't allow myself to see another path, I can assure you I wouldn't be where I am now. It's funny how you get so immensely caught up in everyone else's expectations of you that you fail to stop and think about what you truly want or believe. The only way to move forward for me was to accept and evaluate. Reevaluating everything I'd ever learnt about myself and diving into my tool belt so to speak was how I was able to move forward with 13 Interiors. I needed to take that leap into the unknown and back myself. With 20 years' business experience in different fields, this no longer felt like a sidestep into the unknown. It was a progression to where I was supposed to be, utilising years of experience, my marketing and management skills from setting up swim schools, the leadership skills I'd developed managing large diverse teams, and the communication and quality assurance skills I'd learnt working in mining.

Each of these has become a huge asset to developing 13 Interiors into a company and successful design business. It's easy to get caught up thinking that you need all the design skills to run a successful interior design business when in fact it's only about 20 per cent of the work you'll do as you expand. As my business started growing, I knew the key thing I needed to address was what my role was going to be moving forward. Weird right?

I'd obviously created this business to design people's homes, but I also needed to work to my strengths. I couldn't be everything to everyone – I didn't need to be. This was an old limiting belief that you need to do it all and service everyone in the same way. If I'd learnt anything from life to this point, it was that I couldn't limit my beliefs in what I could do and just because everyone else creates a design business a certain way doesn't mean I need to be doing the same. I hired a successful team who now works with me Australia wide and each of us play to our strengths.

After 8 years of 13 Interiors, I still pinch myself every day that this is something I created. A company that lives and breathes design, that thrives on creating our clients' forever homes and ultimately changing the way they live. I've built a brand that I'm proud of and is truly about creating beautiful functional homes. Every aspect of learning from my life and previous roles is weaved into the success of 13 Interiors. The lessons learnt with change and expectations have created a better version of me. More empathy, understanding, and patience. This has created a successful workplace culture for our team, as I don't let society or industry expectations affect us. We create the narrative and instill that into every project we work on. Through my challenges, learnings and now acceptance, 13 Interiors will only thrive from here with my motto: "You don't have to be everything to everyone… just everything to your ideal client."

The launch of our second studio in Melbourne is a testament to our hard work and dedication, but it's also a beacon of hope for those who may feel lost or uncertain about their future. It serves as a reminder that we can achieve our dreams even if they look different from what we and others expected. My journey wasn't always smooth, but every challenge taught me invaluable lessons about resilience, perseverance, and the importance of staying true to oneself. Though there were uncertainties along the way, I now look back with gratitude at the winding path that led me here and take pride in my accomplishments. Looking back is essential to recognise our growth and be proud of our progress. It's not about dwelling on the past but acknowledging our journey while moving forward with confidence.

Life doesn't have a one-size-fits-all blueprint, and that's the beauty of it. We must celebrate and honour our individual journeys, recognising that they are what make us unique. As I reflect on the moments that have defined my life, I am filled with gratitude for the lessons learned and the people who have been a part of my story. The support of my family, the inspiration from my mentors, and the unwavering belief in my abilities have all been pivotal in shaping my career. And while I may not have followed the traditional path my parents envisioned, I found my own way, one that is rich with creativity, fulfillment and joy.

Moving forward, I am committed to continuing this journey with an open heart and a curious mind. There are still many questions to ask and answers to discover. And in doing so, I hope to inspire others to do the same – to question, to explore, and to embrace the unknown with courage. I want to show you that through the most frustrating and emotionally exhausting times, truly remarkable things can still happen. It takes courage and strength to forge a different path, and I hope that my story gives you hope and allows you to step onto a path that you didn't even realise existed.

To anyone reading this, know that your journey is valid and valuable. Whether you are just starting out, in the middle, or somewhere along the winding path, your experiences matter. Embrace them, learn from them, and let them guide you towards a future filled with endless possibilities. Together, let us redefine what it means to live a fulfilled life. Let us break free from societal expectations and instead, embrace our individual stories and the connections we make along the way. Let us invoke all our senses, create intriguing and complex characters, experience strong emotions, and use a rich and captivating voice to tell our own unique tales. Because it's through our journeys that we can inspire and impact others and leave a legacy in this world. Above all, never forget your why.

LEARNING TO THRIVE

Thrive is the stage where everything you've been growing, through grief, anger, experimentation, and acceptance, finally begins to bloom. It's not a return to 'normal' but the arrival at something far richer: a life that may look nothing like what you once imagined and yet feels more yours than anything that came before. This is where the alternative path transforms from Plan B into the truest version of Plan A – a life built with intention, resilience, and self-defined meaning.

When you're in the thriving stage, it's okay if you feel:

- Free despite the people you may have let down to get here

- Completely fulfilled without guilt

- Happy for the path that got you here

- Unbothered by other people's expectations and feelings

For me, thriving meant stepping fully into the life I'd chosen. I invested in my interior design business not just as a career move, but as a reclamation of joy and purpose. It was terrifying at first, letting go of the identity I thought I'd have, but somewhere along the way, that grief gave way to pride. The business didn't just grow, it thrived. It became my 'baby' in a very real sense: something I nurtured, shaped, and watched evolve into something bigger than I'd ever dreamed. I discovered new layers of creativity, connection, and contribution I didn't know I was capable of.

Thrive is the moment you are no longer comparing this life to the one you thought you should have.

Part of thriving is implementing purposeful strategy for both your life and business. It's your ultimate to-do list. Where the contents of your brain swirls around back and forth and where the influence of our environment can dictate the outcome. If I've learnt anything from my journey, it will always be that the environment and our choices play a part, but it's the why and the strategy that determine success.

Here are a few strategies that help guide me:

- **Goal lists:** Sounds terribly cliché but it works. I have a year planner that I use in Asana where I list out my year ahead and what I'd like to achieve.

- **Achievement lists:** It's amazing how a little reminder of what we have achieved can change our thought pattern and perception. I spoke about comparison earlier in the book and this has been a great tool for me in business and life. A little reminder goes a long way.

- **Boundaries:** For the first time in my life, I have boundaries. Boundaries about the circles of friendships, people I work with, conversations I'm a part of and routines I set for myself. It's about protecting your space and your environment. You are the only person that can do this for you!

FINAL WORD

During a break in Thailand when I began writing this book, I was sitting by the pool one afternoon when a couple enjoying their honeymoon introduced themselves. After asking about our vacation, they directed the conversation to asking me if I had children. I responded no. I braced for the rush of disappointment and grief that usually came, but I was surprised to feel that it didn't. For the first time in a decade, those words flowed easy. I was content with my life choices, the expectations that I'd let go of and the new path I was creating. I'd built my own life, and this one didn't have any limits.

People often say never
look back, but I believe
the power is in looking
back to remind yourself
where you came
from and be proud of
where you're going.

REFERENCES

Excerpts on pages 116 and 124 taken from *The Magnolia Story* by Chip and Joanna Gaines. Copyright © 2016 by Chip and Joanna Gaines. Used by permission of HarperCollins Christian Publishing. www.harpercollinschristian.com.

Tyrrell P, Harberger S, Schoo C, et al. (2023) *Kubler-Ross Stages of Dying and Subsequent Models of Grief*. In: StatPearls. StatPearls Publishing.

ABOUT THE AUTHOR

With over 20 years' business experience across a range of industries, Kelly runs her own successful interior design business called 13 Interiors. Since inception in 2017, 13 Interiors has grown to operate on a national scale with a studio base in Perth, WA and a second studio location in Melbourne, Victoria.

As one of Australia's leading interior designers, Kelly regularly features across a range of media publications and outlets, including *Adore Magazine*, *Home Beautiful*, *The West Australian*, Perth Home Show, Channel 9, Snooze Australia, Summit Homes Group, 6PR Radio, Business Chicks, *Domain. com.au* and *News.com.au*, and regularly presents workshops and demonstrations at design and styling events.

Kelly has extensive experience within the public speaking sector and enjoys mentoring and sharing her knowledge with like-minded individuals who not only want to learn more about interior design, but also to connect through personal journeys and experiences.

ACKNOWLEDGEMENTS

Ted, my husband and best friend. Thank you for your love, guidance and above all, patience. You are my rock in the darkest moments, you make me laugh when you least expect it and I'm excited for whatever our next chapter brings to this wild and crazy life we lead. Love you always.

PERMISSIONS

Excerpts on pages 116 and 124 taken from *The Magnolia Story* by Chip and Joanna Gaines. Copyright © 2016 by Chip and Joanna Gaines. Used by permission of HarperCollins Christian Publishing. www.harpercollinschristian.com.

AUDIOBOOK

Great news! *No Fence, No Limits* is
also available in audio format.
Jump onto your favourite audiobook
platform now and check it out.

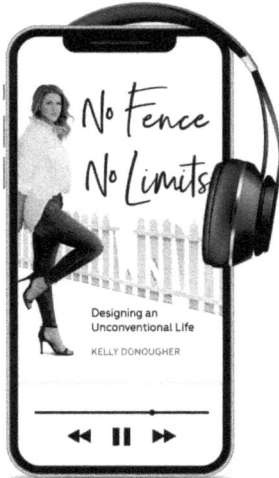

www.ingramcontent.com/pod-product-compliance
Lightning Source LLC
Chambersburg PA
CBHW040925210326
41597CB00030B/5181